The People's His

Women of ᴏᴵᴅ
County Durham

Edited by

Margaret McReady

Workers at Philips' Washington factory in the late 1970s.

Previous page: A Sunderland Corporation conductress in the 1950s.

First published in 2002 by

The People's History Ltd
Suite 1
Byron House
Seaham Grange Business Park
Seaham
Co. Durham
SR7 0PY

ISBN 1 902527 93 3

Contents

Introduction   5

1. In the Workplace   7

2. At Play   39

3. Home and Family   51

4. Wartime   67

5. Hard Times   97

6. A Day to Remember   111

Acknowledgements   126

Mayor of Sunderland Myers Wayman presenting awards to nurses from Ryhope Cherry Knowle Emergency Hospital at the beginning of the Second World War.

All royalties from this book will go to
the charity Breast Cancer Care.

Introduction

As the saying goes 'A woman's place is in the home', but is it? Over the years women's roles have changed and I hope to show in this book just a small insight into what varied and sometimes dangerous occupations women have followed.

During the past century women have proved to be a resilient and versatile section of the community. Life was hard for the ordinary women of old County Durham, but when you meet them and listen to their stories you realise that they were extraordinary in every way, facing life's hardships the only way they knew, which was by making the most of it!

The lives of the women of old County Durham were dramatically changed when war was declared. Whether it was the First World War or the Second, some loved ones left and never returned, but life had to go on. Women's work was vital during the war years whether it be in munitions factories or on the land. Even Lord Haw Haw mentioned the 'Aycliffe Angels' in his propaganda broadcasts.

I consider this book to be a tribute to the hard working, irrepressible women of old County Durham, whose strength of character never ceases to amaze me.

Margaret McReady
November 2002

Dedicated to the Memory of
Pam Gamble

SECTION
ONE

IN THE WORKPLACE

Young girls in the bottling department of Vaux Breweries in Sunderland between the wars. Like many workplaces, girls were expected to leave (or forced to finish) when they got married.

DOWSON BROS.,

VICTORIA STREET, GATESHEAD-ON-TYNE.

Sole Agents for Duncan, Gilmour & Co.'s Non-Intoxicating Hop Bitter Beer.

GENUINE

ÆRATED

WATERS

VIZ. :—

Lemonade,
Gingerade,
Hot Tom,
Ginger Ale,
Ciderade,
Horehound Beer
Soda, Potass,
Seltzer, and
Vichy Waters,
Kola.

D. Bros. wish to draw the attention of the Public generally to their Refreshing Beverages, which are solely under their own superintendence ; their aim being purity only.

N.B.—Parties supplied any distance by rail.

Women workers were always prominent in the soft drinks industry as this advert for Dowson's Factory at Gateshead from 1894 shows.

Women working in the hay fields in Weardale before the First World War.

In his book *Weardale Memories and Traditions* John Lee recalled a number of unsung heroines from 19th and 20th century Weardale. One of these was Hannah English who was widowed early in life and struggled to bring up her young family alone on her farm. 'No sacrifice was too great, no farm work in all its variety too hard or exacting, coupled with that of mending clothes and clogs she could ill-afford to renew ... She toiled to live barely but honestly ... Stockingless, her feet protected by clogs, she toiled in the bed of the stream, at times up to her knees in the water, getting out stones which her bairns carried away as best they could, for her to build walls that would help to make her livelihood a little more secure.'

Right: For some there was the chance to start a new life on the other side of the world as this advert from the *Seaham Weekly News* from 1913 shows.

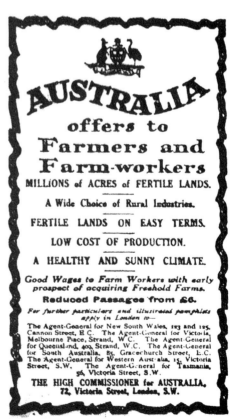

Government legislation in 1945 set up the North Eastern Development Area which covered the whole of County Durham. Industrial estates sprang up all over the county and thousands of these new factory jobs went to women.

Within the first decade of the North Eastern Development Area's creation many large companies built factories in County Durham. These included Patons and Baldwins (Darlington), Siemens (first at Spennymoor and then West Hartlepool) and Ericssons (Sunderland).

A Peterlee town guide from 1956. As Peterlee New Town took shape in the early 1950s one of the stated objectives from the start was to provide industrial employment for women.

I love it here...

...working at Dewhirst's

Miss Christine Elizabeth Honnor, 6 Mann Crescent, Murton, Co. Durham, says...

"Of course I looked round the other factories first, but I liked Dewhirsts so much I decided this was the place for me. And it certainly is—I love it here. The Supervisors couldn't be more helpful; in fact they've brought me on so well that in only eight weeks I'm getting bonus pay. I've made lots of new friends here at Dewhirsts, and when my sister's old enough to leave school, I'll certainly recommend her to come here".

Better Pay
Better Conditions
Understanding Care

DEWHIRST'S
MAKERS OF "ST. MICHAEL" SHIRTS
I. J. DEWHIRST LTD.
Stephenson Road, Peterlee, Co. Durham. Tel. 2256

One of the firms that set up factories in Peterlee was Dewhirst's. From 1884 Dewhirst's supplied garments to Marks & Spencer. In the 1980s Dewhirsts had a total of eight factories in the region. In recent years loss of orders, including the Marks & Spencer account, have led to factory closures and the paying off of large numbers of women workers.

Left: A Murton girl recommends Dewhirst's Peterlee factory to school leavers in this 1969 advertisement.

Machinists at Hepworth's tailoring factory in Pallion, Sunderland, in the late 1950s.

The vast majority of the workforce at Hepworth's at this time were women. The company described how the 'Hepworth touch' was 'achieved in magnificently equipped factories in Sunderland, using new and outstandingly successful production techniques. A happy and united staff of 2,000 work together under ideal conditions embracing the most modern ideas in machinery, air-conditioned, clinical and welfare facilities.'

Right: An advert for Hepworth's from 1957. At this time the factory supplied over 250 shops all round Britain.

BLUEPRINT for PRODUCTION

The Social Service Centre at Grange Villa is adapted as a staff training unit in conjunction with the North East Area Development Scheme.

Local workers are instructed in production of fashion garments and form the nucleus staff for an Industry new to this area.

Work begins on a modern factory site which occupies a central position in Chester-le-Street to provide employment for 500 local workers.

The new premises occupy an area of 23,000 sq. ft. and provision has been made for the inclusion of all up-to-date staff amenities.

Rodney Dresses

(Proprietors:- D. & M. CASH LTD. LONDON. W.I.)

CHESTER-LE-STREET.   CO. DURHAM

The plan for Rodney Dresses factory at Picktree Lane, Chester-le-Street, is outlined in this advert from 1947-48.

London fashion house D & M Cash were drawn to the area by the North Eastern Development Area scheme. Trading under the name Rodney Dresses they first employed 500 workers making frocks and dresses for the export market. As early as the 1960s the working week at the factory finished at 2.30 on a Friday afternoon.

Right: A Patons advert from the mid 1970s. John Paton & Son were founded in 1805 and later went into partnership with J. & J. Baldwin & Partners which had been established in 1785. After the Second World War Patons & Baldwins built a new factory at Darlington at a cost of £7 million.

PICKTREE LANE
CHESTER-LE-STREET

Vacancies Exist

Where you can help to make Rodney Dresses —now worn by women everywhere

YOUNG LADIES

if you are looking for an interesting job, what other can hold greater appeal or give more satisfaction than dressmaking?

SEEING LATEST FASHIONS—

HANDLING NEWEST FABRICS—

All under one roof in a modern factory with ideal conditions

WORKING WEEK FINISHES FRIDAY 2-30 p.m.

Apply
Personnel Officer

Rodney DRESSES

PICKTREE LANE, CHESTER-LE-STREET, CO. DURHAM

Rodney Dresses were advertising vacancies for young ladies in 1964.

The greatest name in knitting........

PATONS

Patons are renowned the world over as producers of knitting yarns and high fashion designs— a service backed by nearly 190 years experience.

Patons & Baldwins Limited,
McMullen Road,
Darlington, Co. Durham
DL1 1YQ

Two ladies being shown how to tie the weaver's knot at Patons & Baldwins in the late 1940s. When the works was built it was the largest knitting wool factory in the world. (Picture courtesy of North of England Newspapers.)

The end of a shift at Patons & Baldwins in August 1950 with the gates still to be completed. (Picture courtesy of Coats Crafts UK.)

" . . . . The garment chosen should be within the scope of, and preferably for the wear of, the makers ; the fixing and making of each garment should be the entire work of one scholar."

Left: This advertisement from 1935 was aimed at schoolteachers but shows how girls trained on such sewing machines would be well suited to go straight into clothing factories.

Spennymoor was described as fashion-leaders in 1971. The Courtaulds factory at Spennymoor opened in the late 1960s and was a major employer of local women.

"... the entire work of one scholar"

● Senior girls understand so much better the value of needlework teaching when—having learned the first steps of hand-sewing in the lower classes—they progress to actual making and mending with a Singer, just as they see it done at home.

Only the Singer Sewing Machine gives the lightness of touch essential to youthful operators—with the sturdy strength sufficient to withstand a long succession of enthusiastic but inexpert little hands.

★ *School Authorities are invited to ask for free demonstration. There are special discounts from List Prices of Machines when supplied for School use. Write for full details to Singer Sewing Machine Co. Ltd., Singer Building, City Road, London, E.C.1.*

In the last few years the region's textile industry has been decimated. Cheap imports and the loss of important home markets has led to companies like Courtaulds and Dewhirst's making thousands of women redundant. A lot of these have found new employment in care work and call centres.

Darlington's Pease's Mill around 1930. Pease's first mill in Darlington began life in 1752. The mill was just one part of the Pease industrial empire which also included iron ore mines, railways and collieries. (Picture courtesy of The Northern Echo.)

The canteen at Pease's Mill in April 1939.

Stockton Market which at one time was the place servants were hired. This took place twice a year – on the last Wednesdays before old May Day and old Martinmas Day. Similar Hirings were held all round the county. John Sykes'

Local Records states that the 6th May 1682 was the first day that men and women servants presented themselves to be hired in Durham Market.

Carlisle Market Place in 1904 showing a young girl accepting a shilling which contracted her into domestic service. It was common for girls from areas like County Durham to find work away from home. (Picture courtesy of Mr J. Templeton.)

A group of staff at Raby Castle around 1935. Kitchen maid Bessie Failes, from Willington, is on the far right. The others include gardeners, house maids and a nightwatchman. Bessie was found work by a nearby agency which would find 'places' for local girls.

Britain's Land of Promise. A week from Liverpool. Golden opportunities for competent agriculturists who can quickly become landlords. Dairying, cattle raising, fruit growing, gardening, unlimited market. 100 million acres virgin soil 2s. per acre —easy terms. Improved freehold farms can be bought for what British farmers pay in rent.

ONTARIO (CANADA).

Grand climate. Thousands of acres in peaches. Ideal educational social conditions. Bright prospects for female domestics. The Government guarantee to place competent men and women. Marvellous natural resources awaiting investors. Write—Mr. N. B. Colcock, Ontario Government Agent, 163, Strand, London. Please mention this paper.

Above: An advertisement from the *Seaham Weekly News* of 28th March 1913. It was offering the opportunity of starting a new life in Canada claiming there were 'bright prospects for female domestics'. What the ad did not say was the work was often on farms and rather than household chores outdoor labour was involved.

Right: A maid at St John's Chapel Vicarage in Weardale taking delivery of a batch of eggs around 1910.

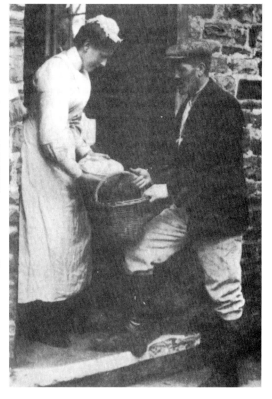

A 16-year-old Broadens Her Horizons
by Murdina Tedder (née Butler)

I left Hudson Road School in 1927 but in those days there was no picking and choosing your job because my mother told me 'Right, get out and take the first job that comes up'.

My first job in Sunderland was to be a house cleaner for Dr Hunter who lived up at Chester Road. My wage was half a crown (12½p) and for that I had to clean the house from top to bottom. It was a back-breaking job but in those days you had to take any sort of work. One strict order made by my mother was that I had to walk up to work from Hendon and back again. I was never to squander even a halfpenny on the tram ride.

At the age of 16 I decided that I wanted to broaden my horizons and enrolled at Mrs Littlejohn's National Domestic Agency in Durham Road. Mrs Littlejohn offered me the chance of working as a housemaid in London which I jumped at. My mother on hearing of my intentions was horrified at the idea of such a young girl setting off to the wicked big city. But I was determined and, with the help of the agency who provided the bus fare plus a future take from the wage, I purchased a ticket to London which cost 10 shillings (50p) and travelled down overnight.

My first job was to be a housemaid for a family called Geffen. Mrs Geffen, as arranged, met me in London and escorted me to the family home at 35 Colville Road, W11. My employer, Dr Maximillian Geffen, was a good boss who ran his practice from his residence. I enjoyed my work there but as with all youngsters I wanted to see more and took up another job offer with a Jewish tailor named David

Price 3d

THE DUTIES OF A HOUSE PARLOUR MAID

Where a Cook-General is Kept.

A booklet for parlour maids.

Wax. Mr Wax lived in Wembley and had a shop in the Mile End Road in East London. The Wax family did not treat me as a humble domestic but as part of the family. Along with another live-in domestic I was invited to attend a family wedding in an East End synagogue and we later joined in the celebrations held at the Grosvenor Hotel.

One day I got talking to another girl from the north who worked as a chambermaid at the Russell Hotel, Russell Square. The girl told me I could earn more working as a chambermaid in hotels so I took up the offer and started work at the Russell. All the girls had to sleep in one big room which was rife with mice. Most of the guests were commercial travellers and on average would leave 6d ($2\frac{1}{2}$p) as a tip.

Murdina Tedder with one of her 13 great-grandchildren. She was one of the many girls who moved away to go into service to escape the hardship in the North East between the wars

I recall two of the chambermaids were also from the North East, one from Easington and the other from Seaham. Both girls didn't like working in London because they were homesick. I told them what was the point of going back home, owing to the slump in the 1930s, there was nothing up there. I told them they should stick it out but they returned home.

In those days staff like me could, and did, work in the south coast resorts in the summer season only returning to London for autumn and winter work. This enabled me to work in places I would never have seen if I had stayed in Sunderland. I worked in hotels in Eastbourne, Hove, Brighton and on the Isle of Wight. Work for women in hotels in those days was so easy to come by. You could walk out of one job and pop round the corner into another.

Every week I used to send 10 shillings to my mother back in Sunderland. She had been widowed in 1926 and if I missed a payment my mother would send me a sharp reminder.

It was while working in a London hotel that I met my husband. His family were from Walthamstow and Plaistow in East London and he was a pastry chef. We were married in 1937 at South Croydon.

With the advent of the Second World War, London and the south became too dangerous owing to air raids. So I chose to bring the family back north while my husband continued to work in hotels throughout the country. Alas he was to die at an early age down south thus severing plans to move back down there. Something which in later life I often regretted.

Workers from George W. Horner's Dainty Dinah factory at Chester-le-Street around 1912. Miss M. Coleman is on the right in the front row.

Horner's expanded in the 1920s opening branches around Britain stretching from London in the south to Glasgow in the north.

At 106 feet high the factory chimney was a local landmark with the words 'Horner' and 'Dainty Dinah Toffee' picked out in tiles.

Left: Miss Coleman can be seen again posing by herself in the grounds of the factory.

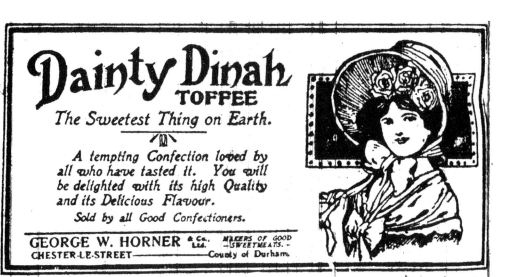

A Dainty Dinah advertisement from 1915 promoting 'The Sweetest Thing on Earth'.

A workers' party at Horner's – at one time one of the biggest employers of women in Chester-le-Street.

The Three R's
by Miss Parkin

I was born in West Roddymoor (near Crook). There are only a few houses left there now. My mother stayed at home and my father worked in the colliery as a colliery boiler minder, at Bankfoot. He worked partly in connection with the coke works and partly with the power station. (The power stations, there were two, provided the colliery with electricity. They had it before the rest of the town.) He worked there all of his life. He had an accident just before he retired which made him an invalid for the rest of his life. He had damaged his neck.

I started school at the elementary school in Crook, and then I went on to the County School in Bishop Auckland. From there I went to St Mary's College, Durham, to study English and German. It was very unusual to go to the grammar school and especially unusual to go on to University. There was very few of us who went. There had to be a lot of parental sacrifice. It was very difficult, even though I was an only child. It was also unusual because I was a girl and there seemed to be a general opinion that education was wasted on a girl: that she would soon get married and that it would be lost. But my parents felt that it was very important for me to have something behind me. I had a very wise father who saw education as giving me an independence. But they had to make sacrifices for me to have such an education. The costs were high and his wages weren't very good.

I spent two years at my first school, which was on the other side of the County at Deaf Hill, near Trimdon. It was a primary school. I wanted to go into a grammar school, but there were many teachers without jobs at all and it was as difficult then as it is today. That was in 1926.

In the early days teaching was parrot like. They had to do a lot of hard graft and learning by heart. It was good on the three Rs. That's

Leasingthorne Village School, groups IV and I, around 1920.

where the main emphasis was. When they left school most of the girls found work in shops, with the occasional one going into an office. There was also domestic work for girls. The boys went down the colliery. The 'cream' had already gone off to Wolsingham Grammar School.

I was teaching during the 1926 General Strike. I was in Deaf Hill and that was a very strong Labour place. The teachers had to help feed the children and we would take them down to the kitchens to see that they had jam and bread in the mornings, and soup at lunchtime. A few men stayed in work ... blacklegs, and I remember being at the boys school then and they all jumped up on their desks and shouted 'Blacklegs' as these men went past on the way to work. You can imagine children doing that today but they did that then. Jumped on their desks ... 'Blacklegs'.

I had my first taste of opera at the Crook theatre. There used to be some good companies. They had full houses. Television has seen the end of the cinemas and theatre in Crook. You have to go to Bishop Auckland to see a film.

When I remember Crook as it was I remember the coke works. The coke works stood out with its big chimneys. There was also a smell over the town from the works. There would be a smell of the coke work fumes in the houses. The closure broke many people's hearts. It saddened the town. It made it a little dead really. The place has become more beautiful since, but that has come through sadness.

I don't always agree with the Council and what they do and say but you've got to hand it to them they have done a lot to beautify Crook. All the pit heaps have been cleared away and where Bankfoot was there are now green fields.

A lot of people moved away when the pits and coke works closed. They went gradually, they didn't all move away in a body. Some saw what was happening and took their chance and moved away. Quite a lot of them went to the Midlands. It was a terrible time for those who had to leave as they had grown up here.

Boarding and Day School for Girls,
2 Ravensworth Terrace, Durham.

This Boarding School for Girls in Durham was run by Miss Gordon with the assistance of resident mistresses and visiting masters. The 1913 advert declared every effort was made to insure 'the moral, mental and physical development of each pupil in the midst of pleasant and healthy surroundings. The school course gives a complete and thorough modern education, and pupils, if agreeable, are, prepared for University, Music, and other examinations.'

For a small minority of girls in Durham private education could be bought at establishments like Miss Gordon's. She charged 30 to 40 guineas for board and education.

An ad from around 1953 showing Ericssons new factory at Southwick.

Workers at Plessey's at its peak around 1970.

When Ericsson moved to a factory on North Hylton Road in Sunderland in 1946 it became a large employer of women. By the 1960s the workforce had risen to over two thousand and there was also a name change to Plessey's. The number employed soared to 3,500 so it was a devastating blow when the factory closed in 1977.

WORKS PASS OUT

CYCLES MUST NOT BE USED ON THE COMPANY'S BUSINESS WITHOUT PERMISSION.

Name.................................... Clock No. ....
Staff No.................

HAS MY PERMISSION TO LEAVE WORKS

REASON..

Period.................................... Date........................
Head of
(Signed)..Department

THIS PASS MUST BE GIVEN TO GATEKEEPER TO WHOM YOU MUST REPORT WHEN RETURNING TO THE FACTORY

FOR ALL OTHER PARTICULARS SEE FACTORY AND STAFF REGULATIONS.
F.1045

BELOW THIS LINE TO BE FILLED IN BY GATEKEEPER.

TIME OUT	DATE	TIME BACK

Ericsson's in 1960, Mary Robinson is on the right.

Pass outs were sometimes used at holiday times to go to No 5 Factory (The Torrens public house).

Above: Ericsson's No 3 Factory in the 1960s. Left to right (first names only): Dora, Mary, Irene, Doris, Jean and Agnes.

Right: Plessey girls enjoying a night together at the La Strada in the 1960s.

Below: A Plessey reunion 25 years after the factory's closure. The event was held at the Roker Hotel ballroom on 28th September 2002.

A Woman's Work Is Never Done

by Lena Cooper

In the 1930s the variety of jobs open to women where I lived was somewhat limited. There was the local brick factory (Lumley Brickworks) which employed women to deal with some of the brick-making processes. In 1935/36 I was told of a vacancy in the office of the Chester-le-Street Co-operative Society Bakery Department. Being advised to apply for the post, I did and got the job. At the time I had no idea what was involved in this. I discovered that my starting time was 6 am and the finishing could be approximately 3 or 4 pm.

My first morning I had to be out of bed at 5 am, dressed – breakfasted and on my way for my 3 mile walk to Chester-le-Street to start work at 6 am. At that time there were no service buses before 6 am – but I started work at 6 am.

Lena Cooper in relaxed mood, around 1945.

When I got to work, my first job was in the office, checking the bakery orders from the various Co-op Branches and taking orders by telephone. When all the orders were written up they were taken into the bakehouse for their attention and packing on to the bakery boards for the vans to do branch deliveries.

My next duty was to stay in the bakehouse and grease tins for that day's batch of pies, cakes etc. The bakehouse was on the first floor and below at the ground level was the tea-room. On odd occasions I was told to service the tea-room. That was where I learned how to make a pot of tea and how to toast a teacake.

After a while I was able to get transferred to Fencehouses Branch in the drapery department. The bakery was to be closed. Nothing to do with me – honest!

So it was much better in all ways – start at 9 am and just a short walk to work. I was about 17 years old and reckoned I only had to put in one year in this job then I could apply to become a nurse, which was what I wanted to be – but I had to be 18 before I could apply.

Working in the drapery department of the Co-op (Fencehouses Branch) was enjoyable up to a point but I hated having to do the chores at home that involved getting my nails dirty!

The worst job – in those pre-war days – was cleaning the 'pit-clothes'. These were worn by male members of the family who worked down the mine at Lumley Sixth Pit Colliery. Each item of clothing was full of coaldust and had to be 'dadded' against the wall in the back street to get rid of this. Then with an old knife the pit boots had to be freed from all the 'clarts' and rubbish that had built up on the sides and bottom of the boots, then greased.

I never understood why it was always my job to do this, just as it was always my job to scrub the scullery (kitchen) and pantry floors on a washing day after I got home from my job at the Co-op drapery department.

Invariably Monday was the day for washing for the whole family. I once tried my hand at 'possing' but it was not easy to lift the 'poss stick' let alone hit the clothes with any downward pressure.

Tuesdays and Wednesdays were for ironing and putting clean clothes away, then the bedrooms had to be cleaned.

Thursday was baking day – with pies, teacakes, bread, scones, sponge cakes, custard tarts, and sometimes jam tarts and small queen cakes. All day was used for baking the food for the family to last for about a week.

Friday was always cleaning downstairs of the house from front door to back yard and occasionally after lunch there was some shopping to be done.

Saturdays were sometimes used for shopping in Sunderland or Newcastle according to how much spare cash was available for items required. This did not happen every week – just once in a while.

The Sabbath Day was kept holy – I went to Lumley Thicks Chapel (long since converted into a dwelling house) in the morning. We went to Sunday school after dinner, then back to chapel again in the evening. This routine lasted until I was 13 when I was confirmed at St Barnabas Church, Burnmoor and began the same routine at the church. This continued until I was 18 and sent in my application to be a nurse. I was accepted for my probationary period and went to Preston Hospital, North Shields, in 1938. I had no idea what I was letting myself in for but it was my ambition and I was very keen. About this time the war clouds were gathering and every nurse would be needed. It was the beginning of a dangerous, yet exciting era.

Lena Cooper (far left back row) with staff and medics from one of the wards at Preston Hospital, North Shields (note the sandbags background) around 1939/40.

Above: The tube production line at Philips factory at Washington around 1977. The works made television components.

Left: Women at Philips in the late 1970s celebrating a special occasion for one of their workmates. Friendships made in the workplace often lasted a lifetime.

A strong contingent of women workers at Ball's (Deptford) Pottery in 1902.

Howard Smith's Wearside paper factory in the 1960s.

A Farming Life

As well as the industrial areas of County Durham there are large tracts of the county devoted to farmland. Here are a series of photographs from Town Farm at Ryhope from the last century.

Horses still being used for haymaking despite being well into the twentieth century.

Some things never change on the farm – such as rearing orphan calves.

The wives and daughters of farmers had busy lives combining their work in the home with helping out with the animals and doing their share in the fields.

At one time farm labourers entered into an agreement with farmers to work for a fixed period of time. In the 1820s the half-yearly Hiring of farm servants was held in front of the Exchange Building in Sunderland in May and November.

In neighbouring Northumberland farm labourers had to provide a woman worker (usually his daughter) as part of his Hiring agreement. These women agricultural workers were called bondagers.

It's clear this woman would not be confined to the farm.

Mrs Clement – Mustard Manufacturer

At one time Durham was at the heart of the nation's mustard industry. This can be traced to a Durham woman called Mrs Clement who perfected a method of mustard seed extraction in 1720. Mrs Clement was not a woman to sit back on her achievement as she travelled the country taking orders for her Durham mustard factory. Her product received a

boost when George I gave his stamp of approval.

Mrs Clement's business passed into the hands of Thomas Troutbeck Ainsley. By the time of the 1883 advert (*above*) he was described as the only manufactory in the city.

Local farmers found mustard was a lucrative crop to grow and a great deal was grown in fields at Houghall.

By the end of the nineteenth century Colman's had acquired the last of the Durham mustard factories. While Colman's are still the leading brand name today the centre of the mustard industry has moved from Durham to Norwich.

Durham's Silver Street at the time Ainsley had his manufactory there and was advertising his wares.

A post woman from the Trimdon area around the time of the First World War.

Fishwives are among those waiting to take a newly landed catch at Sunderland fish quay in the 1930s. Fishwives like these and others from Shields and Cullercoats would travel around the villages of County Durham selling their fish.

TOWNS Commercial School & Copying Office.

SITUATIONS BUREAU.

Baltic Chambers,

John St., Sunderland.

'Phone: Sunderland 2160.

Above: An advertisement for copy typists from 1929.

Right: This advert from the Situations Vacant section for a Sunderland mail order company shows the wage rates for copy typists in 1969. An 18-year-old could earn £8 17s a week, 19-year-old – £9 7s 6d, 20-year-old – £9 17s and 21 and over – £11 3s 6d. In addition there was a bonus scheme and welfare and canteen facilities.

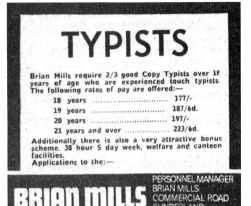

On the Buses (& Trams)

The First World War led to labour shortages on the tramways. In June 1915 Sunderland Corporation Tramways employed its first ten conductresses (although they were known as conductors at this time). By the end of the conflict the whole of the Tramways' fleet had conductresses on board.

Women also replaced men on South Shields Corporation Tramways during the war. By the spring of 1917 there were thirty-six conductresses as well as women cleaners in the tramsheds.

The work of women on the tramways was not without its

Sunderland Tramways' conductresses during the First World War. The sign in the tram window reads 'Eat Less Bread'.

dangers – apart from the odd assault by passengers or having things thrown at them by boys – they had to deal with attacks from the air. On the 1st April 1916 during a Zeppelin raid on Sunderland a tram received a direct hit from a bomb. The conductress, Margaret Ann Holmes, was severely injured in the incident and had to have her leg amputated. An inspector and 22 passengers were killed by the bomb.

Most women were 'retired' after the war to allow the return of men. However, Miss Holmes, after spending months in hospital recuperating, returned to work at the Tramways offices until she retired in 1950.

A conductress taking fares on the top deck during the First World War.

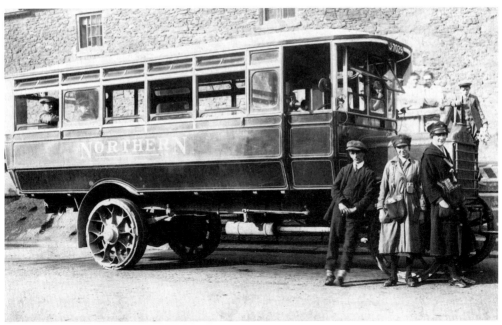

As buses replaced trams conductresses became accepted as not just a 'wartime necessity' – these are at Consett around 1923.

Nora Varty seen here as a young 'clippie' in the 1940s for ABC – named after its proprietors, Messrs Arron, Binks and Coulson. This well known bus company ran for many years around the Ferryhill area.

Sunderland Corporation bus conductress Nan Nash in 1956.

The Ropery on the corner of Fulwell Road and Roker Avenue was for a long time one of the few large employers of women in Sunderland.

Above: The end of an era – the final Ropery buildings being demolished.

Left: Two Ropery Girls in the 1930s.

A cutter hard at work in the Ropery in the 1960s.

A Ferryhill Woman in the Air Force

In 1947 Doris McLean from Ferryhill joined the Women's Auxiliary Air Force and did her training at Wilmslow in Cheshire. Details from her copy of *Notes For Recruits and New Arrivals* gives a glimpse of what it was like on an RAF Station in the late 1940s.

'When you are proceeding along any of the roads in the Station, you should always be properly dressed and present a smart appearance. Greatcoats when worn, should be buttoned up with collar turned down.

'Pay particular attention to your clothing, look after your kit, and send your boots and shoes for repair at the proper time – don't wait until you are down to the uppers.

'Keep yourself clean in person as well as your clothing; ensure that you have a hot bath at least once a week and keep your hair properly cut and tidy.

'Facilities are available on Station for you to enjoy most sport. I would like you to take advantage of these opportunities by contacting

Air Craft Woman Doris McLean (now Predki) in 1948.

your Physical Fitness Officer, who will no doubt also be able to arrange for you to take part in sports other than those already catered for by the Station.

'We have a Station Cinema which shows all the most up-to-date films.

'Dances are held on Station, and particulars of these are always given well in advance on Orders and through the medium of the Station Notice Boards.

'Are you interested in play-reading, dramatics, discussion groups, or have you any particular hobby? If so, contact the Education Officer, who will be pleased to include you in these activities. Further details are to be found in Station Routine Orders and also broadcast over the Tannoy.'

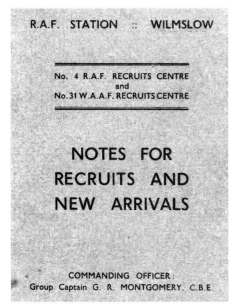

R.A.F. STATION :: WILMSLOW

No. 4 R.A.F. RECRUITS CENTRE
and
No. 31 W.A.A.F. RECRUITS CENTRE

NOTES FOR
RECRUITS AND
NEW ARRIVALS

COMMANDING OFFICER :
Group Captain G. R. MONTGOMERY. C.B.E.

A presentation in the early 1970s to Nurse Bessie Lowes for twenty-five years service as a Ferryhill midwife. Margaret Greenland is seen here handing over a bouquet of flowers. Jean James is holding her son Mark. Also included are: Suzanne Greenland, Stephanie Varty and Julie Fox.

Traffic wardens in Sunderland in the 1980s.

AT PLAY

Shotley Bridge Spa

Victorian ladies taking the waters at Shotley Bridge Spa (*left*). At this time the spa waters were famed for their medicinal properties. The spa was credited with many miracle cures. One report said an ailing woman regained her colour and vigour after taking the waters for a few days in 1837.

Below: Women, children and a pet dog enjoying a day out at Shotley Spa grounds in the last century.

A Trip from Seaham to Whitby

On 18th July 1870 a steam paddle-ship trip left Seaham Harbour for Whitby. The *Seaham Weekly News* reported the *Vigilant's* progress: 'In parts of the boat singing and dancing are being indulged in. Others again are discussing the contents of the innumerable baskets which contain the provisions. Judging from the hilarious laugh and the good-humoured chaffing that is everywhere heard all is enjoyment – the everyday cares have been forgotten and happiness reigns undisturbed, save to those who are troubled with that monster sea-sickness.' When the Seaham day-trippers disembarked at Whitby they broke up into parties to visit the sights. After a good day at the seaside the party returned safely to Seaham. The newspaper noted 'every one of the excursionists enjoyed the trip and wished from their hearts that the promoters may have another next year.'

Public Notices.

LONDONDERRY RAILWAY WORKSHOPS'.

TRIP TO WHITBY.

The Steamer will leave the harbour at 6·15 on Monday morning first.

The *Seaham Observer* advert for the excursion to Whitby in 1870.

Circus Time

The arrival of the circus was a great time for the population of local towns and villages. These photographs show the circus parade at the bottom of Roker Avenue in Sunderland early in the last century. The circus would arrive on railway trucks and disembark at Monkwearmouth Station. They would then proceed down Roker Avenue then along the seafront to Seaburn where they would set up the big top. Bertram Mills Circus was a regular visitor to Sunderland.

Lord George Sanger's Circus was another that paid regular visits to County Durham in the early 1900s. Among the attractions for their Good Friday performance at Seaham in 1905 were: Twelve Japanese Wonders (turning lofty somersaults), camels, horses and a herd of great elephants.

Ha'Way The Lasses

by Lily Brett

County Durham has been described as England's richest soccer nursery but passion for the game in the region can also be said to extend to ladies' football. A major factor in the rise in the popularity of women's football was the First World War.

The large number of females employed in munitions works led to women's football teams being formed. These, combined with teams from other industries, led to a flourishing fixture list. Games were held all over the county – teams from Darlington, Hartlepool, Birtley, Ryhope and Sunderland all played each other. These sides also ventured across the Tyne to play in Willington Quay, Newcastle and Blyth.

In Sunderland the rope-making industry produced a number of women's football teams. These included: Glaholm and Robson's in Hendon, Webster's Ropes in Deptford and Craven's Ropery in Monkwearmouth (who were known as Sunderland Ladies). Sarah Ryles, who captained Sunderland Ladies, recalled how they also played against men's teams. 'The men didn't go all out but we were quite capable of giving them a good game.'

The popularity of football in the First World War was not so much because of the increase in the number of women in the workplace but the move from jobs in domestic service, shops etc into munitions works and heavy industry. The large munitions works put thousands of

A girls team that played a Darlington side in November 1917. On the ball is their name 'Expansion'.

Birtley Cartridge Case Factory football team in 1917-18 season. The team's home games were played on Chester-le-Street cricket ground.

women together in one place of work for the first time. Of the 11,000 women at the Gretna National Cordite Factory 36% had been in domestic service, 20% had lived at home and 17% had been shop assistants, laundry workers, dressmakers, school teachers or clerks. This in turn led to organised sports for the workers' spare time such as football. A publication of one National Projectile Factory called *Bombshell* reported on matches at the works in June 1917 and reflected: 'Who would have dreamed two years ago of women playing football?'

The footballing friendships forged in those wartime factories continued after the war ended. This was seen when Ryhope Munition Workers' women's football team were still playing under this name more than two years after the end of the war. In June 1921 Sunderland Ladies beat Ryhope Munitions Workers 3-1 in a game to raise money for 'feeding the bairns' and collected over £10. On the same day Silksworth met Monkwearmouth Ladies and over £12 was raised for the soup kitchens in both areas. A few days later Ryhope played Silksworth before a crowd of 10,000 raising £16 11s 6d for charity.

The interest these games generated led to Mr F. Bloom offering a shield for a competition between the women's football teams of County Durham. The teams who entered included: Washington, Bankhead, Ryhope, Felling, Silksworth, Wardley and Wearmouth. Silksworth ran out winners of the competition and were honoured at a ceremony at the local Miners' Hall at the end of August 1921. Mr Bloom presented the Silksworth captain, Mrs S. Wolfendale, with the shield and handed out gold medals to each member of the winning team. On their way to victory they had raised £72 for local relief funds.

At the Seaside

Crimdon Dene was a popular seaside destination for many folk in the county. Some families used to take most of their furniture from home for their stay in the chalets.

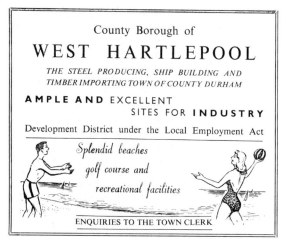

In an attempt to attract new industries to West Hartlepool in the early 1960s the area's beaches were used as selling points. In recent years the coastline has been cleaned up after years of pollution. The beaches are unrecognisable from the days when Blackhall Beach was used for the final scene in the classic film *Get Carter* – chosen for its bleak industrial outlook.

Nora Robinson and son Jimmy on the golden sands of Seaburn Beach in 1954.

At one time the Big Dipper was a familiar sight on the Seaburn skyline. It closed down after a fatal accident in 1970. Three years later the Big Dipper was demolished.

A young boy enjoying one of the rides at Seaburn Fair in the 1950s.

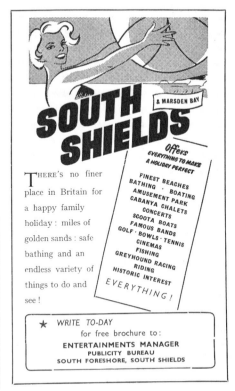

An advert from 1955 extolling the virtues of South Shields and Marsden Bay.

Two pictures from a Sports Day at the Girls County School, Bishop Auckland, in July 1936.

Sports Days were always special occasions in the school calendar. The egg & spoon and sack races of infant children were no less keenly fought than senior competitions like those above.

Sadly for most girls their schooldays were the last opportunity they had to play organised sports. While boys continued with sports like football through works' teams, church sides or at sports clubs there were few such outlets for girls.

Left: What the best dressed female was wearing for sporting activities between 1884 and 1930.

The Girl's Own Paper from July 1894.
The penny price might still have been
too much for some girls.

An advert for Houghton Feast from
1975, one of the region's oldest
surviving events.

Members of the Salvation Army with a group of Life-Saving Guards. General
Bramwell Booth authorised the formation of Life-Saving Guards in 1915,
influenced no doubt by the Girl Guide Movement which had started five years
earlier.

Wolsingham ladies in Victorian dress for a dance in 1925.

The Troubadours Concert Party, Elizabeth Wilkinson is second front row, third left. Elizabeth and Bert Wilkinson started up the Troubadours in 1932 and toured Durham and parts of Northumberland. Bert (christened Isaac) Wilkinson grew up on a farm near Butterknowle but when he was twelve moved to South Shields when his father Jack was recruited by Harton Colliery Band. This was one of the top bands around and one of their highlights was winning a silver medal at Crystal Palace.

Mary Failes (left) washing up at a Day Centre in St Margaret's Hospital, Durham, in the early 1960s. Old people would often go to the day centre to do crafts.

Mary Robinson at Roker Park in June 1997 shortly before the old stadium's demolition. From the 1940s onwards Mary had followed her favourites there. Mary achieved a remarkable success in 2001 with the publication of her book *Barbary Coasters* about life in Monkwearmouth. In her seventy-fourth year she had written a best-seller! Mary donated all her royalties from the book to St Benedict's Hospice.

Mowbray Park with its duck pond has always been a popular attraction for Wearsiders. The old Winter Gardens can be seen in the background of this picture. They were pulled down after being badly damaged in an air raid during the last war. Today a new Winter Gardens is pulling in the crowds.

Girls enjoying a game in Backhouse Park, Sunderland, in the 1950s.

HOME AND FAMILY

Monday Was Washing Day

by Margaret Ann Henderson (née Mallon)

Everyday housework had to be done and like most people Monday was washing day and my daughters Margaret (Peggy) and Nora were always there to help. I had to get up early in the morning to light the boiler in the wash house and when the water was hot enough the washing would be started. I always insisted that the clothes were soaped inside and out, and sometimes my daughters would try to lessen their work by just soaping the outside before putting the washing in the poss tub. 'Woe betide us if my mother finds out.' I heard our Peggy say, 'She'll never know if we put the washing straight into the

Washing day in the back yard of Woodbine Street, Hendon, in 1948. Myself (right), daughter Peggy and niece Theresa (front).

Reckitts' blue bag was a familiar sight on wash days.

poss tub' replied our Nora. 'She's the cat's mother, and she will know if you don't soap inside and out, lady' I said as I walked into the wash house. Needless to say the clothes were washed properly after that – I think! It took a whole day to do the washing, from lighting the boiler, soaping (inside and out!), scrubbing the clothes, putting them in the poss tub, wringing them out with the mangle, and then the ironing with the flat iron not forgetting the 'dolly blue' for your whites!

The poss stick mill at Ebchester. The stacks of wood seen beside the water wheel shows the mill's output was considerable. The outfit of the lady on the stepping stones suggests the picture was taken around the time of the First World War.

T. SILL,

Sole Manufacturer of

Sill's Patent ::
:: Possing Stick,

SPECIALITY:

Wholesale Cabinet and General Wood Turner,

VILLIERS STREET,
West Hartlepool.

ESTIMATES FREE.

NATIONAL TELEPHONE 505.

An advert for poss sticks manufactured by a West Hartlepool firm just before the First World War.

This advert from the mid 1950s shows one local laundry's efforts to gain new customers. Health and safety might not have been high on the average housewife's list of reasons to send out her laundry.

Let Hot Water do the Work

Rubbing and scrubbing won't get the grease off pots and pans, plates and dishes, unless you have a good supply of really hot water.

Probably a dozen times a day you need hot water for this or other purposes.

You can easily meet your needs by installing a gas water-heater. Soon fixed, it puts an end to hot water supply troubles.

We offer free expert assistance in solving your heating, cooking, water-heating, lighting and power problems— in making your home "a home of comfort," and in increasing the efficiency of your office, shop or factory. Write or call to-day.

Seaham Gas & Lighting Company.
Office & Showroom: 19, North Railway Street
Seaham Harbour.

Above: Fairy Soap has been an essential household item for many years. This advert comes from the 1940s during the days of rationing.

Right: An advert for 'hot water at your finger tips' from the *Seaham Weekly News* in 1930.

Super OXYDOL

GIVES MORE LATHER - CONTAINS NO BLEACH!

SPECIAL NOTE: Make sure you tell your shopkeeper it's Oxydol you want on your ration. He can now get enough Oxydol to supply everyone who asks for it.

Above: Another product from the ration era but unlike Fairy Soap this brand has not survived to the present day.

Left: One of the advertising slogans of this 1930s brand was 'Let Rinso wash while you sleep.'

Right: The result of all those wash days – these women and children are in Sunderland East End around 1900.

THE SHINING NEW Duo-matic

the wash-rinse-spin combination
with every star feature you ever wanted!

Never before such a galaxy of star features in any washing machine—at any price!

TWO automatic pumps to do all the filling, emptying and tub-to-tub transferring; table-tray cover; non-spill stream-lined top; RUSTLESS alloy cabinet; CHILD-PROOF SAFETY BRAKE plus new LEVER-LOCK SPINNER SWITCH; huge twin tubs; new SNAG-FREE SPINNER without sidewall perforations; UNIQUE SPRAY RINSING; automatic time switch; TWO super-silent motors to work spinner and washer independently; latest pulsator giving famous "turbo-boil" action—and a host of other wonderful features!

All this, plus 2 YEARS' GUARANTEE and 2 YEARS' FREE MAINTENANCE backed by nation-wide "flying squad" service fleet and a first-class after-guarantee service too! Without a shadow of doubt, this is far and away the greatest combination washing machine you can buy—

YET ITS CASH PRICE IS ONLY

52 GUINEAS

...or £11.12.0 deposit and
10/2 WEEKLY FOR 2 YEARS

—BECAUSE IT'S STRAIGHT FROM THE FACTORY AT FACTORY PRICE!

Amazing new stainless steel safety heater unit (entirely optional extra) 10 gns. **NO HIDDEN EXTRAS!**

BRUCE FORSYTH says
"Drop me a coupon and find out all about the Shining New Duo-matic"

FREE ILLUSTRATED BROCHURE sent by return
To Duo-matic Ltd., Dept. R.T.10, Victoria Road, Romford, Essex
Please send me your free brochure by post

NAME ....

ADDRESS ....

.... R.T.10

L DELIVERY FROM YOUR LOCAL BRANCH ┘

ADA THE HOME LAUNDRESS

PRICE £57.6.8 including purchase tax

ADA says
"HERE'S A PICTURE OF HAPPINESS TAKEN ON WASHDAY!"

Happy to be free from back-aching drudgery, happy to see how gently, thoroughly ADA's swish-swirl action coaxes out the dirt, happy to have the power-driven 12-inch rollers to do the turning—adjust pressure at a touch of the finger—ADA does the rest. This home laundress has the sturdiness and capacity needed for a full family wash—entirely rustproof throughout, ADA is built for life-long satisfaction. Write today for picture folder and name of nearest dealer to **AJAX DOMESTIC APPLIANCE CO. LTD., Dept. U, Halifax, Yorks.**

Above: An advert from 1949 for a washing machine to rid housewives of 'back-aching drudgery'.

Left: Bruce Forsyth endorsed this twin tub in 1960 for 'only' 52 guineas cash or £64 9s 4d over two years.

Even when washing machines became more readily available after the war many families could not afford them and had to continue washing the old fashioned way.

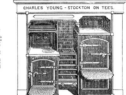
Above: A Stockton firm advertising the latest in cooking technology in 1876. Ranges like these could be found in County Durham homes well into the following century (*left*).

Nora Varty and Murial Carter deciding to dress up as 'Odd Job Girls' in Conniston Road, Ferryhill, 1939.

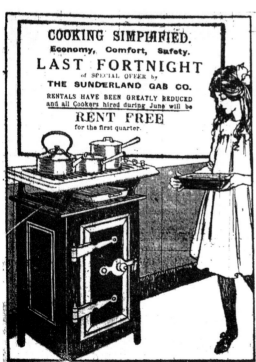

The latest in gas cookers in 1913.

Harrison's Buildings in the East End of Sunderland overlooking the cranes of the docks and shipyards. They were the town's first council houses. Built in 1903 to replace the slum dwellings of the notorious Hat Case area. The budget for the project began to escalate and the plans had to be modified. As a cost-cutting measure the flats would no longer have their own baths as originally intended.

The back yard of a house in Whickham Street, Sunderland in the 1930s. The zinc bath tub hanging on the back wall shows there were still no bathrooms for many local households thirty years after Harrison's Buildings were built.

Childhood Memories
by Dorothy Jameson (née Pearson)

Every little girl loves to dress up in pretty dresses but in my case it was more than the dress that was special.

My father, Lesley Pearson, was a window cleaner in the 1940s and one of his clients had a business in Frederick Street, Sunderland. One day while he was cleaning the windows he stepped back (to admire his work, so he told me!) and fell to the ground. As the buildings in Frederick Street were the high Victorian terraced style he sustained serious injuries.

It took a long time for my father to recover from his accident as he had broken practically every bone in his body. He was given physiotherapy to help his recovery. As the bones in his hands had been

Me outside Great Aunt Harriet's in Kayll Road, Sunderland, wearing one of the dresses my father embroidered.

damaged he was given special exercises to do, this was to learn embroidery. I can just try to imagine the determination it took just to be able to hold the fine embroidery needle never mind the patience to actually thread the needle!

I was so proud of my dresses that my father had embroidered for my sister Margaret and I. Some had balloons embroidered around the hem and others had pretty rows of flowers. We wore our dresses to church on Sunday and when we attended Sunday School at Christ Church.

It must have been a worrying time for my mother, Lillian Pearson, but my father persevered with his exercises and eventually made a full recovery.

Me with my mother, Lillian Pearson, and the stag's head that my Uncle Tom insisted joined us in the photograph!

CHURCH STREET, WEST HARTLEPOOL.   H.9195.

Mothers pushing their prams in Church Street in West Hartlepool. This was an age when prams were a regular feature on the county's streets. Today this is a rare sight with prams being replaced by buggies.

One of the busiest times for pram manufacturers was after the Second World War. The number of babies born in England and Wales jumped from 679,937 in the last year of the war to 820,719 in 1946 and 881,026 the following year. These numbers were not reached again until the 1960s.

Right: An advertisement for perambulators from 1886. Interestingly there were 903,760 births in England and Wales in this year – higher than in the years of the baby boom!

59

An Edwardian scene of ladies outside Lambton Castle. The young boy in charge of the horse appears to be dressed in his Sunday best!

Mr and Mrs Newton from Ferryhill who over many years fostered children. Here are just three of them, left to right: Christina, Morgan and John.

A Durham Man in Mesopotamia
by Margaret Ann Henderson (née Mallon)

When I met John Henderson in the days before the First World War he was a rifleman in the Durham Light Infantry. Little did I know when I met him it would be almost a decade before we would be married. He was sent out to Mesopotamia (now modern day Iraq) early in our courtship. He served nine years in the army and on his return we married. The two special gifts he brought home for me were a brooch made from a bullet cartridge and a shawl.

Right: My husband serving in Mesopotamia. He brought the shawl home as a gift for me.

Below: John and I when we were first married. The brooch in my blouse was made from a bullet shell.

The Co-operative Society

The Co-operative Movement began in Rochdale in the 1840s but soon spread to County Durham. The Co-ops kept prices down by manufacturing their own goods and producing foodstuffs on their own farms.

The opening of Rookhope Branch of the Stanhope and Weardale Co-op early in the twentieth century. It appears quite an occasion with everyone dressed in their Sunday best.

A Birtley Co-op advertisement from 1913. In the late 1870s and early '80s the Birtley Society opened branches in Washington, Wrekenton, Ouston and, in 1901, Pattinson Town (chemical works). By 1926 the Birtley Society employed 245 people, ran one car, 5 vans and lorries as well as 47 horses.

An advert for Crook Co-op from just before the First World War. Crook Society started in 1864 in a building rented from the landlord of a local public house. It opened for business in August 1865 and they bought their first horse and cart for deliveries the following month. Other stores followed and the society prospered – reaching sales of £³/₄ million by 1920.

Staff pose outside the Easington Branch of the Haswell Co-operative Provision Society. In the 19th century even organisations like the Co-op did not treat their men and women employees equally. In 1890 the Annfield Plain Co-op's minimum weekly wage for Grocery and Drapery countermen, Butchery salesmen and Rolleymen was 24 shillings. This was three times as much as Hardware and Drapery saleswomen and Millinery trimmers received. The maximum wage for these jobs was still twice as much for men than women. Male clerks received a minimum of 24 shillings compared with Female clerks who only got 6 shillings. The maximum wage of these rose to 28 shillings for men and 14 shillings for women. Even Boy clerks received 8 shillings rising to 24 shillings. In 1894 the heads of the Hardware Department at Annfield Plain branches started at 26 shillings (male) and 12 shillings (female) rising to 32 shillings (men) and 16 shillings (female). Even for seemingly egalitarian businesses some of its workers were more equal than others.

Barnard Castle Market Place was an important meeting place for those from the more isolated parts of County Durham.

The barrow boys in Sunderland doing a flourishing trade.

The market in Union Street in Sunderland was set up on the bombsite of the Empress Hotel which had to be demolished after being damaged in an air raid in the Second World War. Street market traders – 'barrow boys' – took advantage of bombsites like these in the town centre to set up their stalls. They were popular with customers because they did not need ration coupons to buy their goods. The slow rate of the post-war rebuilding programme allowed the barrow boys to continue on bombsites many years after the end of the war.

Wolsingham Market on the 10th June 1904. The occasion was the re-opening of the market.

From rural communities in the west to the industrial conurbations in the east, County Durham has a rich and varied cultural heritage which is reflected in the different dialects and various terms for the same thing within the county. In his book *Life and Tradition in Northumberland & Durham* Frank Atkinson noted: 'Ask someone from Sunderland what he asks for when ordering a helping of fish and chips at his local shop. If he was born and bred in Sunderland he will probably ask for *a fish lot*. Someone from Gateshead would probably ask for *a paper* and somebody from Stanley in West Durham would probably ask for *a fish and bag*. And there are other words associated with this delicious food such as *scraggins* from Shildon.'

GEORGE PICKERING,

SILK MERCER

AND

DRAPER.

COUNTY HOUSE,

CHESTER-LE-STREET.

George Pickering's impressive drapery establishment at Chester-le-Street in 1879.

Left: An advertisement from the late 1940s for Broughs grocers at Chester-le-Street.

In the 1890s J.W. Brough would send his salesmen into the mining villages of County Durham to take orders and then make the deliveries. Broughs became a serious rival to the Co-op in these areas. In the early 1900s there were depots at Gateshead, Stanley and Crook and by 1914 Broughs had branches in Spennymoor and Chester-le-Street.

Below: Church Street in Seaham continues to be at the heart of the town's shopping.

WARTIME

Munition Workers

When the First World War began men left industry in huge numbers to join the Armed Forces leaving gaps in the workforce that women went a long way to fill. Early in 1915 there was a shell shortage and Lloyd George was made the first Minister of Munitions and it was with the help of women that he was able to solve the shell crisis. Women played a major role in the munitions factories and many of them were set up in the region in places like Birtley, Darlington and Dipton. One of the largest was in Gretna which employed 11,000 women and many of these were County Durham girls living in hostels.

FOOD FOR THE GUNS.

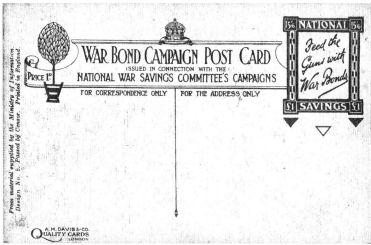

The front and back of a postcard showing women workers in a shell factory during the First World War. It was issued to promote National War Savings. The illustration had been supplied by the Ministry of Information and had been passed by the Censor.

Working in the munitions works was a hazardous job both from the chemicals used to made the ordnance and from the continual threat of explosions. The worst incident took place on the 19th January 1917 at Silvertown in East London when a fire set off 50 tons of TNT. The huge explosion flattened a square mile of the capital. The blast killed 69 people (a further four died later) and injured 450. A dozen women workers were among the fatalities but the death toll would have been much higher had it occurred in normal working hours. The devastating blast happened in the evening and much of the area had been cleared after a warning.

A First World War poster calling for women to go into munitions works. Many of the women who went into the ordnance factories were the wives of soldiers and sailors doing the fighting.

When Canaries Had No Reason To Sing

Apart from the constant danger of explosions, working in munitions factories had many other health hazards. Contact with explosive materials turned workers' skin yellow and such women were called 'canaries'. One writer recalled seeing a train full of munitions workers at a station. She said their skin was stained a 'yellow-brown even to the roots of their dishevelled hair by the awful stuff they handled.'

A report in the *Lancet* from 12th August 1916 described the effects TNT had on women workers. These included: throat and chest problems, coughing, sometimes a thick yellow phlegm; abdomen pain; nausea; vomiting; constipation at first, then diarrhoea; skin rashes; giddiness; hot and cold flushes; drowsiness; memory loss; sight disorders; delirium; coma and convulsions.

Dipton Munition Workers

In November 1917 a service was held at St John's Church, Dipton, for the local munitions workers. A local newspaper reported: 'The vicar (Reverend R. Tuson) gave a short address to the munition girls of Dipton on their splendid response to the country's call. Having signed over 300 papers for admission of girls to the works, he said girls were still going to make munitions, and that all honour was due to those who had helped the men to the path of victory.'

Birtley National Projectile Factory

The munitions factory at Birtley during the First World War was extraordinary because the workforce was comprised almost entirely of Belgian refugees. A shell and cartridge factory was already being built at Birtley when it was decided the Belgians, seeking refuge here after their country was invaded, should supply the labour force. This in turn led to the construction of a small town to house the workers and their families. The complex of huts accommodated 5,000 people and was named Elisabethville in honour of the Belgian Queen.

Workers at what is believed to be Birtley Munitions Works in the First World War. Note the flowers in the shell casings.

The Ministry of Munitions Journal of July 1917 reported the comments of a general manager of one of the National Shell Factories about his women workers:

'They are willing and cheerful; they sing at their work, and are immensely keen to get as big an output as possible. Many a time have I noticed chalked on a machine a message from the girl who has been operating that machine during the day to the girl coming on to it on the night shift, a challenge-like message somewhat as follows: "120, Lizzie! Beat that if you can, and let me hear from you!"

'I have actually known of girls, who, because their machine may have broken down for a short time, or perhaps because a batch of hard steel has come through, shed tears because their output has fallen short of that of the girls at adjacent machines.'

Workers in Darlington Shell Shop in 1915. The lady on the right in the front row is Miss Maggie Laycock.

Above: Women cleaners at Shildon Engine Sheds in 1918.

In the summer of 1914 the railways did not employ any women engine cleaners. By July 1918 there were 3,065. The total number of women employed on the railways rose from 12,423 before the war to 65,887 in 1918.

Right: Women workers at Darlington around 1915. During the First World War the North Eastern Railways' Darlington workshops housed an emergency shell factory. The vast majority employed there were female – one thousand women in a labour force of 1,150.

Women workers at Teams Hy-Product Coke Company's Works during the First World War.

Like many works, women had not been employed in large numbers at this Tyneside firm until the war. High wages in factories at this time attracted many women from low paid jobs such as those in domestic service.

WHO WILL SERVE THE COUNTRY?

RECRUITING SERGEANT. "NOW, BRAVE BOYS, WITH THOSE WHISKERS AND SHOULDERS YOU SHOULD BE WITH US, AND——I'M SURE THE LADIES WOULD EXCUSE YOU!"

WE'LL SERVE THE SHOP.

The First World War was by no means the first time women replaced men in the workplace in times of crisis as these illustrations from *Punch* show. The conflict in question was the Indian Mutiny of 1857.

Military personnel convalescing at Stanhope Sanatorium during the First World War. The servicemen are dressed in their 'hospital blues' alongside sanatorium staff.

England's enemies, Huns, hoarders, and heedless housewives

A poster warning housewives of the effect U-boats were having on food supplies during the First World War. Many County Durham families always grew their

own vegetables in gardens and allotments (*above*). There were shortages of certain foodstuffs – and at times queuing – but rationing was only introduced in the final year of the war. National Kitchens were set up all over the country which provided cheap meals which many working women took advantage of. The price of food doubled in the four years of the war.

The Day The War Came To The Hartlepools

A series of postcards producted after the bombardment of Hartlepool and West Hartlepool by German warships in the First World War. On the 16th December 1914 the cruisers *Blucher, Moltke* and *Seyditz* fired hundreds of shells on to the towns. While the target might have been the dock area and gun battery, many houses were hit and over one hundred civilians were killed. Among the victims in Lily Street were Polly (23) and Jane Ann (17) Cornforth and Elizabeth Agnes Harper (49) from Moor Street. Another 500 men, women and children were wounded in the attack.

The Women's Land Army

The shortage of agricultural workers during the First World War led to the formation of the Women's Land Army. They replaced men on farms and in forestry work. By the end of the war there were 113,000 women working on the land. The Women's Land Army continued on for a full year after the war ended.

Even before the Second World War began, recruitment to the Women's Land Army had started with men again having to be replaced on the land.

While some might have thought this was an easy alternative to factory work in reality many of the Land Girls had a hard life. In winter they were out in snow, rain and hail for 48 hours a week. In summertime their working day was even longer having to make use of all the daylight hours. Many lived in hostels or on isolated farms with little or no entertainment.

Land Girls had their own distinctive uniform consisting of green pullovers, brown breeches or dungarees, brown felt hats, shirts, rubber boots and khaki overcoats. When these wore out they often reverted to ex-army issue uniforms.

Some of the Land Army's tasks included: ploughing, milking cows, looking after animals, picking fruit and vegetables, clearing scrubland, hedging, chopping down trees and rat-catching.

A group of Land Girls in County Durham during the First World War.

'Why, Joe—not finished yet?'

When you suddenly find you've mastered the job you've been learning, and can pay back some of the friendly teasing that went with your tuition—what fun it can be, on a farm! In an office, it isn't quite the same. ' Still typing that letter, Sheila?' wouldn't get much of a laugh . . . It's the difference of working as one of a small, skilled farm team whose members know each other and help each other: where the boss of the farm is one of the team too. One of those little differences that, for the right woman, can help to make life on the land the happiest job of all.

JOIN THE WOMEN'S LAND ARMY

Post this **COUPON** for further information	To Womens Land Army, Dept. 15H , 6, Chesham St., London, SW1. Send details, please
	NAME..
	ADDRESS...
	.... (Use 1d. Stamp—unsealed envelope)

Issued by the Ministry of Labour and National Service in conjunction with the Ministry of Agriculture

Above: Two Land Girls outside Darlington in 1948.

Right: A recruitment ad for the Women's Land Army from 1949.

A group of Land Girls near Sadberge, outside Darlington, in 1947. The girls were clearing scrubland.

Hendon Memories

by Margaret Ann Henderson (née Mallon)

When I look back on the war years I often smile and think of all the things we all had to do to make do and mend. Obviously there was rationing and everyone tried to share what little they had if they could. Where we lived in Hendon in Sunderland, it was quite a normal occurrence for me to make a big pan of soup, feed my family and send a large bowl to my neighbours for their meal as well. One day my daughter Nora came in from work with a 'bright idea'. One of her workmates told her that her family mixed their ration of butter with their ration of margarine and it tasted lovely, so out came a bowl and we mixed what was left of our ration of butter and margarine. When it came to the 'tasting' it was quite horrible! Nora kept her 'bright ideas' to herself after that!

We often listened to the wireless as we did not have television in those days. Unfortunately our evening around the wireless was sometimes spoilt by German propaganda messages. One night as my family gathered round for their evening of music and entertainment Lord Haw-Haw came over loud and clear. 'What with your stuttering King and your knock-kneed Queen' he exclaimed to all. Well, I saw red! After everything we were going through, air raids and rationing and he had the nerve to criticise our King and Queen! I was so angry I picked up the clean water bucket and threw the contents over the wireless. 'That's put pay to him!' I said. 'And to the wireless!' replied my daughter Nora, 'But I suppose it could have been worse, it could have been the dirty water bucket!' The wireless did eventually dry out and we did keep the clean water bucket a safe distance away after that.

Food Rationing made front page news on 2nd November 1939.

'Don't dance about on it, Winnie, you might fall through.'

The lighter side of air raid preparation could still be seen in this cartoon from an issue of *Punch* in October 1939.

A woman Air Raid Precautions Warden at work during the Second World War. It was the warden's job to ensure the black-out was enforced. They were also trained to fight fires after bombing raids with stirrup pumps. In the early years of the war one warden in every six was a woman.

Workers outside the camouflaged-roofed Grangetown Box Factory in Ocean Road, Sunderland. All but nine of the 171 staff in the picture are women. The majority of these lived in Seaham, Deneside, Ryhope and Silksworth. The factory made shell cases in the Second World War and men from the Royal Ordnance Factory at Birtley helped train some of the women.

Evacuated To Toronto
by Joyce Carlson (née Wilkinson)

My father was born on a farm outside Butterknowle and moved to South Shields when he was twelve when his father got a job with Harton Colliery Company in 1928. He was an excellent musician and played in the colliery band. This was very lucky for us as I had lots of relations in the country to visit. My father married a South Shields girl and after my brother and I were born we often had family holidays in the country. We used to book a cottage at least once a year for a week. I used to look forward to the farm teas. In those days farmers' wives would set out a table in their parlour and serve home-made tarts, cakes and tea to passers-by.

As well as these holidays I was often sent to stay with relatives in the school holidays. My mother or father would put me on a bus at Newcastle and ask the conductor to make sure I was put off at the appropriate stop, where a relation would be waiting to take me home for a week or two. One of the places I went to was Toronto (about one and a half miles from Bishop Auckland) where my Uncle Jim and Aunt Meg had a poultry farm with about one thousand hens – all free range. They were locked up in large huts with nesting boxes and benches every night but the next morning they were let out into a large open pen where they scratched about very freely with lots of space to wander about. Battery hens were unheard of but in 1939 there was talk of two farmers having their hens in wire cages. The idea was met with disgust from the other farmers including Uncle Jim. No one dreamt that this cruel practice would be quite common in years to come.

When the war broke out in September 1939 I was going to be evacuated along with loads of other children from the North East but Aunt Meg sent a letter to my mother to tell her they would take me into their home for the duration of the war (which everyone was saying would be over by Christmas). So of course I was back to Toronto with two suitcases filled with my belongings. I had my own room and as usual my aunt and uncle were very good to me and, looking back on some

Elizabeth and Bert Wilkinson with daughter Joyce and son Albert in the back yard of 20 Alma Street in 1931. Albert went on to have a very successful fish and chip shop in Moffett Street, South Shields. Joyce went on to become an artist, exhibiting in the Laing Gallery, and the co-author of five books on Shields and one on Jarrow, under her married name of Carlson.

stories of evacuees, I was very lucky. However, the local culture was very different and living there was not like being on holiday. I still had the same friends when I'd been there previously but now I had to go to the local school which was very different from the one I went to at home. At Mortimer Road School in South Shields the teachers were very nice and one, Miss Shields, would play the piano

Joyce Wilkinson, aged 10, at the door of 34 Bewick Street in 1938.

on Friday afternoons when I and some of my friends would sing at the front of the class. We would then go around the other classrooms and 'give a little song'. One of my songs was *A Tisket a Tasket* which was sung by Ella Fitzgerald. The teachers in Toronto Village School were totally different and were very severe and strict. The only singing we did was with the rest of the class and we sang songs such as *Jerusalem*.

Aunt Meg thought my hair, which was cut in what was called a 'bob', would go longer without having to be cut if it was very short. It was cut nearly to the top of my ears and the fringe was so short it was only half an inch long. My mother had always kept me quite fashionably dressed but the clothes I'd brought were put in the drawers in my room and kept for best. Aunt Meg thought they were too good to wear. I was dressed in the old clothes of Aunt Meg's daughter who was a lot older than me and these clothes must have been more than twenty years old. I wore a skirt which was about five inches below the knees and old Wellington boots.

My mother came to see me the week before Christmas to bring me my presents. Later she told me that she had been shocked by my appearance. After Christmas I wanted to go back home but I felt guilty about my aunt and uncle who had been very kind to me – they just lived in a completely different world to me. Just before Easter my mother suggested I should come home because an air-raid shelter had been built in our yard. There also hadn't been any raids for weeks. I agreed to go home but I tried to sound a little bit reluctant in my return letter. So three days before Easter, Aunt Meg took me home by bus. She told my mother that I'd been settled until it was suggested I come back to South Shields. I hadn't been settled of course and I was dying to get home and see my friends and family – but that was not Aunt Meg's fault.

I came home to find that school was now only open for a half day. My school at Mortimer Road did not have its shelters built so we went to Cleadon Park School for half a day. I sat the eleven plus after Easter but even though I had been in the 'A' class all the time I, and none of my classmates, passed. With all the disruption because of the war we had not studied the subjects the questions were based on. At the time I wasn't bothered because I felt that I'd been moved about too much in that six months. However, in years to come, I realised that not going to the high school was a disadvantage but in those days nobody was too concerned as we had the war and its horrors to think about.

Spennymoor nurse Winifred Hall and her National Registration card during her time working at Ryhope Cherry Knowle Emergency Hospital during the Second World War.

Staff at Ryhope Cherry Knowle Emergency Hospital.

Work started on Ryhope Cherry Knowle Emergency Hospital in September 1939 and was opened in May 1940 just in time to receive 200 wounded evacuees from Dunkirk. *Above*: Military patients and staff at the hospital.

In October 1940, 200 women patients were transferred from London's East End to the hospital to escape the Blitz.

Ryhope resident Jack Hedley recalled: 'Nursing staff employed at the hospital during the war years were either conscripted from the Civil Nursing Reserve and employed as nursing auxiliaries, or as assistant nurses with either Red Cross or St John Ambulance training.'

The hospital was later renamed Ryhope General Hospital.

Four members of the hospital's nursing staff taking a break.

The Summer of 1940
by Jane Wooton

In 1940 the old life style began to change. Men and women were put to work in ammunition factories and my dad was one of the many Southwick men sent to work in Coventry.

Jane Wooton.

My friends and me tried unsuccessfully to join the Land Army. It turned out that we were exempt as our work on the farm was considered vital to the war effort, and so the summer of 1940 found us back on the farm as usual.

Each of us would take it in turns to walk up to the big house to get our orders for that day. One day the boss was waiting for us in the tractor shed. He said 'Well lasses we're getting the Army here sometime this week, and if any of them steps out of line, or says or does owt wrong you tell me. From now on the tractor shed is out of bounds because that's where the lads will be sleeping – Right, away lasses into the cow house and help the men clean it out.' Our faces dropped. Home all winter to the cows was a huge open place with two five bar gates with drinking and feeding troughs. By the end of the day the aroma that hung about us and on us didn't invite the companionship of fellow bus passengers, so we walked home and let God's clean air work the necessary miracle.

All that week we worked hard getting the place ready and by the time we got to work the following Monday the soldiers had arrived. The tractor shed had a large notice pinned to the door, 'Out of Bounds', as did the granary. We were a bit miffed about this as the buildings had been our makeshift canteens when we had our bait and cans of tea. Anyway a compromise was found and we settled for the dairy.

Dinnertime was a happy affair with lots of singing and dancing and the odd cigarette or two. We bought the penny song sheets along with a packet of five Woodbines from Jimmy Connor's the newsagent. We even found time in that hour to teach ourselves dances like the Charleston, rumba, foxtrot and quickstep. Our singing and dancing was a source of great amusement to the soldiers. If the soldiers had any time to spare they were more than willing to pitch in and help with the harvest. This made for a good convivial atmosphere all round.

The boss told us to show them how to stook the corn. A binder would first cut and tie the corn into bundles, around the field all neatly laid out would be the corn, wheat and barley patiently waiting for the human touch to complete the job. When full size, a stook of corn consisted of 12 sheaves. After doing this we had to make sure that they were all the same, completely uniform in shape and size and all had to face Penshaw Monument on parade as it were. No matter which field we were working in we never lost sight of our grand view of the Monument – and we certainly didn't need lights to draw our gaze to it.

Wartime Memories
by Ann Nora Robinson (née Henderson)

As I was born in 1925 my teenage years were spent at the beginning of the Second World War. It isn't until I look back at those times that I realise how Hitler stole my youth as well as that of thousands of other teenagers throughout the world. Fortunately I can remember the good times as well as the bad and often smile at some of the incidents that happened.

Nineteen-year-old Ann Nora Robinson.

One of the most important things you had to have with you at all times was your gas mask. Although you hoped you would never have to use it you took it with you everywhere. One day I was out shopping in Fawcett Street with my friend Vera Devine when Vera tripped over a gas mask. 'Someone's lost their gas mask!' exclaimed Vera and promptly kicked it into the gutter. After we had finished our shopping which wasn't very much later as most things were rationed we headed off back home. It was then Vera realised something was missing – it was her gas mask! We practically flew down Fawcett Street. Luckily for Vera her gas mask was still lying in the gutter where she had kicked it. But even though she never lost her gas mask again she never lived the story of her mask down.

Vera and I were practically inseparable and we often went to the pictures in our free time. We were always aware of the dangers of bombings and there was quite a bit of bomb damage in Hendon and the East End of Sunderland. So on this particular night we were on our way to The Villiers (with our gas masks!), when we heard machine gun fire. We were told if ever we heard any machine gun fire to lie face down so there was less chance of being shot. When it became quiet again we continued on our way only for it to start again, again we lay face down until it stopped. As there was little light because of the black-out we always walked close to the walls of houses. Then for the

OFFICIAL INSTRUCTIONS ISSUED BY THE MINISTRY OF HOME SECURITY

GAS ATTACK

HOW TO PUT ON YOUR GAS MASK

Always keep your gas mask with you – day and night. Learn to put it on quickly. Practise wearing it.

1. Hold your breath. 2. Hold mask in front of face, with thumbs inside straps.
3. Thrust chin well forward into mask, pull straps over head as far as they will go.
4. Run finger round face-piece taking care head-straps are not twisted.

third time we heard machine gun fire but then it dawned on us what we thought was machine gun fire was in fact the rat-tat-tat of my belt buckle on the corrugated-iron sheeting surrounding a bombsite. When we arrived at the pictures we could not believe the state our coats were in, we were black from head to toe from diving to the ground to avoid the 'gun fire'.

Aycliffe Angels

In 1940 work began on a huge munitions complex at Aycliffe costing a staggering £7 million. When it opened in the spring of the following year thousands of women from South West Durham, Teesside, Darlington and Durham City were shuttled in by train and bus.

The work was highly dangerous and involved putting powder into shells and assembling detonators and fuses. It is not known how many were killed in accidents but one incident alone claimed eight lives.

It was Lord Haw-Haw who gave the women the name Aycliffe Angels when in one of his broadcasts from Germany he said 'the little angels of Aycliffe will not get away with it.'

Durham University did a study of former Aycliffe workers documenting their wartime experiences. As a result of this research in the mid 1990s *The Northern Echo* started a campaign to win recognition for the role these women played in the war effort. One of those approached was Tony Blair as his Sedgefield constituency was one of the prime recruiting grounds for the factory. He and his agent agreed the women deserved recognition and when he became Prime Minister it was one of the first things he promised to rectify.

In 2000 a Commemoration Service was held at Durham Cathedral to honour the local Home Front efforts, especially the Aycliffe Angels.

Women workers (with a solitary male) in front of one of the 1,000 buildings that formed part of the Royal Ordnance Filling Factory at Aycliffe. (Picture courtesy of The Northern Echo.)

Some of the 17,000 people who at one time worked at Aycliffe – the vast majority of whom were women. The average age was 34 although one thousand were over 50 years old. Many of the girls went to the factory when they were 18 because their mothers did not want them to join the forces. (Picture courtesy of The Northern Echo.)

The Home Front Commemoration Service at Durham Cathedral. From left: Patricia Kirkbride with her mother, 'Aycliffe Angel' Betty Slack from Crook, and right, another 'Aycliffe Angel' Norah Greenwood. (Picture courtesy of The Northern Echo.)

Life at Aycliffe Royal Ordnance Factory
by Ruth Vickery

I was at Aycliffe Royal Ordnance Factory for about three years, I think I started in August 1942 as a Labour Manager having been at Risley ROF (I'm Durham by adoption and I wouldn't swap it for anything). All the other ROFs had hostels for the women workers but when we came up to Aycliffe we didn't want a hostel because there were so many women who could travel in. People were brought in by train and by buses from the pit villages; right round by Bearpark and the north west and so on. At one time they did wonder whether to open a hostel at Aycliffe but they decided not to. I think probably it was a decision that was fair.

We had them from 18 plus onwards, including married women and in total we had about 17,000 there. We worked three shifts – we liked to have the younger ones on three shifts. Where two shifts operated we would have the older ones, perhaps because they were mornings and afternoons there. The great problem was the shopping. They could probably manage with Granny going out – but we had lots of Grannies who came and worked! One of these was Mrs Dillon. We didn't recruit women over 50 and she said she was 49. She was in fact 69 but she was a young-looking 69. Mrs Dillon was awarded a decoration and received it from the king. She told me 'When I got to him I didn't know what to do; the tongue stuck to the roof of my mouth and I said "God bless Your Majesty".'

Workers at Aycliffe ROF around 1945. Back row from left: Mrs G. Preston, Mrs W. Tebble, Miss M. Marley, Mrs E. Hahn. Front row: Mrs L. Woodhouse, Mrs E. Shute, Mrs D. Avery and Mrs Bland.

The Shifting House at Aycliffe where workers discarded their ordinary clothing and put on safety wear. Workers also had to leave behind items such as matches, jewellery or anything that could cause a spark.

Working with detonators was a dangerous job and there were a number of accidents. The youngest girls were put on jobs like these because they had the dexterity. Accidents could happen when more than one detonator was put in at once as it only needed an impact to set it off. I can remember one child having lost both hands. There was always a very thorough investigation and I sat in watching and listening. It was my job usually to go to the hospital to see the kids. Years later when I was working at Patons a 15-year-old girl came to see me. She said 'You know me Mam'; I said 'Do I?', she said 'Yes, she worked at Aycliffe with you: both of her hands were blown off. Said you'd know her if I told you I was her daughter'.

There were a number of people with hands blown off. Sometimes, you never knew the cause, it might be a kirby grip – if they weren't wearing their turbans properly – it might fall in, if they were shovelling detonators or if they weren't looking quite at what they were doing.

I remember the girls who used to work with yellow powder. It got everywhere, whatever precautions you took. It wasn't so much dangerous as disfiguring: it coloured the skin, it coloured their clothes. I think they were very 'front line', even more than on the detonators, which went off so easily on impact.

When a person was ready to come back and they had lost, say, a thumb or a finger or they had injury on their eye or something, we reckoned that we could fix them up with a job – bit of a 'bobby job'.

Compensation for accidents was ridiculous and sometimes they had to wait a long time. Another thing was when they got a sum of say £1,200 – it represented nearly a million to them – and they would blow it! One of the jobs that Mr Bird had to do would be to talk to a person or family, say, if a man had died: he'd say to the wife, 'Don't spend it now; put it into savings certificates'. But they couldn't resist spending it and of course all the hangers-on, like they do with the people who win the pools now: all the hangers-on again. And it was gone, in no time.

We had the Queen Mum visit Aycliffe. We raffled a pair of her shoelaces in aid of the Red Cross. They raised £2, which was an almighty sum in those days. Yes, she was an absolute winner even in those days. The King didn't come, of course, but she was such a natural person.

I really think that shift work did gnaw at your vitality you know and every now and again you just needed to have time off. Housewives had, now and again, to get the house clean. Shopping was also one of the problems: if you were on mornings – the early turn – you hadn't got time to shop, or rather the best things would have gone. If you were on afternoons it was the best shift to do it, and nights, well you could manage but you did it at a price. Yes, and we didn't stop to have

Some of the huge workforce at Aycliffe Royal Ordnance Factory. Most of the buildings had blast-proof mounds around them to confine any explosion.

holidays; I'd nip to Gretna Green and have two days off. You used buses because you couldn't use cars then.

Near the end of the war as POWs were being released many, many of them came home to County Durham. A lot of the DLI were picked up in May and June 1940 at Dunkirk. And in no time, because Durham's very sociable, everybody wanted parties and what better than to invite the POWs. The parties were held in the canteen but they didn't do the catering, though they may have produced something. The women came in with buckets of eggs, half buckets of bacon, rationing or no rationing, they got them. They must have had smallholdings. I'd never seen cream like that – none of us had; and they baked the most fabulous cakes. Perhaps the chaps got extra rations? We had been told you must not feed the POWs on rich food – too much for them – but that didn't deter them. And these chaps came in – and they were bemused, you know, they didn't know what was taking place; and you know, they had lost a big slice of life. They'd been home on leave for a bit – we were very lavish with our leave at that time; it was very good when anybody's son came home. I shall never forget those POW parties; it was usually afternoon shift – it was a dead loss as far as production was concerned – these buckets of food; they came from Willington and so on – it was super; they really turned themselves out.

The Price of Working at Aycliffe

The constant danger of explosions was always hanging over munition workers. A number were killed in explosions at Aycliffe – in one accident eight workers lost their lives. As well as fatalities some lost their sight, limbs, fingers and thumbs in blasts. Working with the toxic chemicals associated with the armaments industry had its own dangers:

'Then they came and asked me if I would go on Group 2. Now Group 2 was where all the powder was done and all my hair went yellow, all up my arms went bright yellow, you would just think I had jaundice – oh it was terrible, real yellow.'

Mrs Batterham

'I was like a buttercup – my face turned yellow as well, and I never had much time for social life at all. By the time I got home, went over to see how Joan (her daughter) was, if she was alright, put things right for the dad to go to the pit and everything – and that, it was nearly time to get up again to go back to work again to get the bus at half past four. I never had much time, but actually when I saw myself in the glass I felt awful about it.'

Lottie Brennan

'Well it didn't suit me really – we were yellow, absolutely yellow – our hands and faces were dreadful. Actually I got married and I had a baby and the baby died so whether that had anything to do with it I don't know. The baby was still-born.'

Mrs R. Fisher

A Wheatley Hill Woman's War

by Esther Meechin

I was born in 1921 near to Wheatley Hill Colliery. My da was a miner and my family moved to 15 Pyman Street when I was only a few weeks old. I was the sixth child. Hannah was the eldest and there was Isabel, Doris, Wilf, Tom, me and then Margaret and Jean were born. We lived at Pyman Street for 15 years. We thought that we were really posh because we had our own ash closet at the bottom of the yard. The residents of nearby streets had to use communal ash closets that were situated in back lanes. They were horrible and smelly. In about 1936 we moved to a new council house at 2 Henderson Avenue. There wasn't much work for women and

Ma's family name was Briggs and she is pictured on the right with her sisters in about 1910.

Some of my brothers and sisters in 1930. At the back, left to right: Hannah, me, Tom and Isabel. Front: Jean and Margaret. Our Isabel became a teacher but she had to leave the profession. Married women weren't allowed to teach in those days.

girls in the pit village and I stayed at home to help ma with the housework. Ma's sisters would visit us and often say: 'Send her to place.' Which meant send her in to service as a servant for prosperous families. They even put pressure on ma to send our Isabel to place instead of her going to teacher training college, but our Isabel wasn't having any of that.

I was happy at Wheatley Hill but the outbreak of war upset things. At the beginning of the war I followed many other Wheatley Hill girls into service. The owners of the big house where I worked in Staffordshire were canny and the mistress bought me a bicycle because it was a long way to the nearest town which was Hanley. Direction signs had been removed and it was difficult to find my way in the area. My hours of work were from 6 am until 8 pm, six and a half days per week and all for 10 shillings and sixpence. My room and meals were included but I had to pay for my own laundry. Looking back it was slave labour but that was the way it was in those days and I just got on with it.

My brother Tom in Pyman Street in 1935. At the end of the row of pit cottages on the right was the railway which connected Wheatley Hill Colliery to Thornley Colliery. There was no fence and we just stepped over the lines to get to the houses on the other side.

On my half day off work I used to travel on my bike to visit my sister Margaret who was in service nearby. She worked for an Army officer and his wife. Margaret did most of her work in the cellar scrubbing and washing the laundry by hand. It was heavy work and her hands were in a terrible state. They were red, swollen and chapped and she couldn't work with her hands anymore so she had to leave her job. My mistress let our Margaret stay at the house with me while her hands healed up. I thought that was really kind of her. Margaret returned home to Wheatley Hill to completely recover and she then went back into service at another house.

Our Margaret (left) and I on one of my visits to see her while we were both in service in Staffordshire in 1941.

I was employed as a parlour maid and served at table. During my first week one of the guests cracked a joke and I smiled. I was immediately followed into the kitchen by the mistress who rebuked me because I hadn't to be seen taking notice of what the guests were saying. Other staff in the house included scullery maid, kitchen maid, two gardeners and the cook/housekeeper who was in charge. But she was bossy and she didn't seem to like me so I moved to another house in Staffordshire. I left the first house on good terms and the mistress let me keep my bike. The second house was about ten times bigger than the previous one and I was employed as a housemaid. The other staff included a butler, footman, gardeners and the cook/housekeeper who was really lovely. The wages were a little better here. Several of the rooms had been closed owing to staff being called up for war service. I liked singing while I worked and on one occasion I was scrubbing the steps leading to my room when the lady's maid told me that the lady of the house had said that I must stop raising my voice in song. I felt embarrassed about that.

Esther Meechin in 1943.

By mid 1941 I had been in service for about one year when I received a letter from my sister Isabel who was with her husband Jack stationed at Dunfermline with the RAF. She had recently given birth and she asked me to go and stay with her because Jack was being moved to Blackpool. I was really pleased to receive that letter. I didn't like being in service but I couldn't afford the train fare back home to Wheatley Hill. Our Isabel sent me the train fare to Dunfermline and I travelled to Scotland during the night. The carriages were dark owing to the black-out and it was a long frightening journey.

I made very good friends with Nancy (left) from the Middlesbrough area and Margaret from County Durham at the munitions factory in Staffordshire.

After several months with Isabel I received a letter from my brother Tom who said I had to return home to register for essential work for the war effort. I signed on at the Wheatley Hill office of the Ministry of Labour and National Service. I had a choice between the Land Army and a munitions factory. I chose factory work and early in 1942 I started work at an armaments factory at Newton Aycliffe where we made bullets. Buses were laid on to take us to and from Wheatley Hill. After about six months many of us were transferred to another factory in the

Esther Meechin is pictured kneeling third from the right with some of the women who lived in the hostel at Drake Hall, Staffordshire. They were all employed at a munitions factory nearby.

Staffordshire countryside near to Stoke-on-Trent. The factory was camouflaged with a grass embankment and it just looked like a big hill in the countryside. The workers made big bombs and bullets and I can still remember the strong smell of chemicals when I first entered the factory for a medical. It made me feel sick and I turned white. The doctor did not pass me fit enough to work in the shops making bombs and I was given a job cleaning out and checking the condition of boxes used to store bullets. I wasn't exposed to chemicals in that factory and I was glad about that. The complexions of the girls employed in bomb making turned yellow and I felt sorry for them. I also saw some big men lose a lot of weight. I worked

The ironing room facilities for the residents of Drake Hall.

The Christmas party dance at Drake Hall in 1943. Esther Meechin is at the extreme left dancing with a serviceman.

three shifts including night shift and I was well paid. I was able to go home to Wheatley Hill to visit my family twice per year and I looked forward to that.

About one mile from the munitions factory was Drake Hall which was a purpose-built communal living hostel where I lived with hundreds of other women who were employed at the factory. Drake Hall was brilliantly organised and we were well looked after. The meals were excellent and there were all sorts of activities, sports and entertainment laid on for us. Every week a dance was organised and servicemen stationed nearby were invited. At first Army, Navy, RAF and American servicemen came on the same night but there was trouble and fights so they were separated and given their own nights. I worked on munitions until the end of the war and Drake Hall was my home for three and a half years. The management told us we could go home when Germany surrendered but I didn't receive a thank you letter for my service never mind a war medal.

I returned home to Wheatley Hill and helped ma with the housework again. In 1950 I married my long-standing boyfriend Jimmy Gibson, a shipyard riveter from Sunderland. Jim wanted us to marry years earlier but I wasn't very keen because of the war. And then there was a housing shortage during the post-war years. I moved to Sunderland but it was noisy and lively after the quiet life at Wheatley Hill. It was a culture shock which took some getting used to. We had four children but Jim died in 1972. I still live in Sunderland today.

HARD TIMES

Born in the Workhouse
by Ethel Dickinson

Life in the 1930s was a lot different than it is today. The welfare system was a very harsh regime and families had a very hard time when money was short. If you needed any type of help the 'Parish' would come to your house to see what you could sell before they would give you any help.

When my mother found out that she was expecting a baby she had no alternative but to go to the Workhouse in Kayll Road, Sunderland. As my mother was one of a large family there was no room for her to stay at home.

I was born in 1934, in the Workhouse, and I was placed in the creche while my mother worked. At this time all the children were in one large room which was full of cots and beds but that was changed later as the staff realised that if any of the children were ill that it wouldn't be long before they were all infected.

Although life was hard in the Workhouse my mother always told me that there was always good nourishing food as there were vegetable plots at the back of the buildings where vegetables were grown for the residents and fresh bread was delivered everyday.

When I was sixteen months old my mother was told about some accommodation for rent at Deptford. We soon moved into the one room that was above a pie shop. As well as accommodation our new home also provided a job for my mother. When she started work in 'Geordie's

One of the buildings that formed Sunderland Workhouse in Chester Road.

Pies and Peas' shop she explained to the owner that she could not leave me alone whilst she worked in the shop. This did not prove a problem; my mother could take me to work with her! So, when my mother went to work so did I. 'Geordie Pies and Peas', as my mother referred to him, made me a cardboard box to sit in while my mother worked. When it came to my meal times I

The regimentation at meal time can be seen at St Pancras Workhouse around 1900. Meals at Sunderland Workhouse might have been better than most as it had its own vegetable plots at the back of the building.

was given a plate of mince and potatoes so I was obviously happy with the situation. When 'Geordie Pies and Peas' asked my mother to marry him my mother declined and decided it was time to move on.

My mother's next job was at the Eye Infirmary when it was situated in Stockton Road. One of her jobs in the kitchen was to count the cutlery! One day there was a spoon missing and my mother searched high and low for it, she asked different members of staff if they had seen the missing spoon but no one had. When my mother asked one of the porters if there was anywhere else she could check for the missing spoon he suggested looking in the incinerator. Not realising what was also put in the incinerator my mother climbed up the steps and put her hand in the collection box only to discover the parts of patients removed during the operations carried out in the Infirmary. Needless to say my mother left that job!

When my mother began to look for another job my grandmother came to her aid. Someone my grandmother knew needed a housekeeper so the next day my mother went for her interview. The gentleman concerned asked various questions and one of them was 'Can you make ginger pudding?' My mother being desperate for the job told him that she could so she got the job and was told to start the following Monday. Everything was going quite well until my mother was asked to make ginger pudding for the next day. But not to worry, my mother went to my grandmother's and told her the problem. My grandmother went to the kitchen and made a ginger pudding for my mother to take with her the next day. Unfortunately, as ginger pudding was the favourite dessert of my mother's employer my mother had to leave, as my grandmother could not face a life of making ginger puddings!

But as domestics were always required my mother soon found another post, this time it was in a sea-going captain's house. Her duties were mainly housework and when the lady of the house, on her way out to friends for the afternoon, told her to clean out the china cabinet she did so. But as the china was very fine and delicate my mother broke a cup and a saucer. So, with the lady of the house being out she went to my grandmother's and again she saved the day by telling my mother to glue the china together and place it at the back of the china cabinet. On returning to the house my mother repaired the china and continued with her cleaning. On the top of the china cabinet there was urn that held the ashes of the daughter of the house. When my mother picked it up to clean it it slipped from her hands. Again she ran to my grandmothers house, my grandmother went to the coal fire, took some fine ashes from the grate, put them in a paper poke and told her to place the ashes in the urn and hand her notice in when the lady of the house returned!

Even though my mother seemed rather accident prone she was still a hard worker and different jobs always seemed to come along. The money was very poor so there was always a need to keep your ears and eyes open for any job no matter how small. My grandmother was always telling my mother of different jobs that people wanted doing, but the one I do remember was the cleaning job in the synagogue in Ryhope Road.

Staff at Sunderland Workhouse around 1930.

My mother took me along to the synagogue which she had heard needed a cleaner. When we arrived the Rabbi told my mother that the synagogue needed cleaning from top to bottom and that the tap for the water was on the first floor. When the Rabbi left my mother had a good look round, leaving me to sit by a little square pool of lovely warm water. I took off my shoes and socks and sat with my feet in the pool and as I was only about three and a half years old I was quite happy sitting there. While I was sitting by the pool my mother asked me where the tap was for the water. I told her it was 'upstairs'. My mother had no intention of carrying buckets of water all that way as she was only being paid two shillings and sixpence and she had promised me a treat out of that! So my mother used the warm water out of my 'paddling pool'.

After a while my mother had finished her work and the Rabbi returned. When he saw that my 'paddling pool' was almost empty he asked where the water had gone. My mother explained that she had used it for the cleaning of the synagogue. At this the Rabbi practically exploded 'That was holy water!' My mother took her money and we left. When we got outside my mother said to me 'I don't know why he was so annoyed, as it was holy water so much the better to clean the place with!'

Christmas In The Workhouse

Throughout the county in the nineteenth century Guardians, local businessmen and civic dignitaries laid on treats for Workhouse inmates. At Darlington Workhouse in 1879 Christmas dinner comprised roast beef and plum pudding. The Mayor and local tradesmen gave inmates tobacco, snuff, sweets and oranges. The Licensed Victuallers' Association provided beer for the occasion. When the Mayor (Mr Swinburne) announced he would give a similar dinner on New Year's Day it was received with a chorus of cheers.

Working Outside The Workhouse

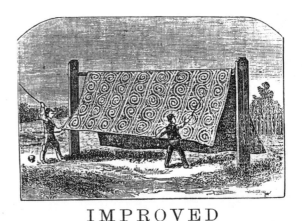

IMPROVED
CARPET DUSTER,

For supporting the Carpets while being beaten; thereby preserving the Seams and Texture from being unduly stretched or torn.

N.B.—A GRASSY LAWN FOR BRUSHING & FOLDING ON.

Keeping the carpet clean 1870s style. Gateshead Workhouse allowed some of its inmates out to beat the carpets of townspeople in 1871.

Lanchester Workhouse

The Cottage Homes at Lanchester around 1900. At this time Poor Law Guardians were taking pauper children from Workhouses and putting them in Cottage Homes to improve their quality of life.

In the nineteenth century the Workhouse system was based on the idea of 'less eligibility'. This meant conditions in the Workhouse were made much worse than conditions outside. This insured the institution was the last resort for people.

The Lanchester Workhouse served a large part of the north west of County Durham. In her book *Lanchester in Times Past* Lilian Dixon wrote about Lanchester Workhouse. It had a vagrants' ward where tramps could get a night's lodging in exchange for performing a task before leaving the following morning. Queues would form outside the gates late each afternoon. Once admitted they would receive bread and water. This meagre diet did improve as the years went by but was still pretty basic – bread, cheese and tea.

Lilian Dixon recalled: 'These tramps – men and women who went from one workhouse to another, were often people who had seen better days. One Lanchester lady can remember a tramping woman who knocked at her mother's door and begged to be allowed to play the piano. She then played a difficult piece from memory with considerable skill, showing she had been brought up in very favourable circumstances.'

In later years the Workhouse became more humane with children going into Cottage Homes for a less institutionalised atmosphere.

By the First World War Lanchester had become less of a poor house and more of a hospital for the elderly. After the Second World War it became Lee Hill Hospital.

The Temperance Movement and The Poor

Christmas has always been the time when attention is drawn to the poor of society. Various groups and individuals in the nineteenth century tried to help those less fortunate than themselves.

The local temperance party in Bishop Auckland used to lay on treats for poor children at Christmas time. On Christmas Day 1879 320 poor children were given a dinner of roast beef, potatoes and plum pudding. Then each child was given a current bun and an orange.

On Christmas morning 1897 a breakfast for 530 poor children was held at the Temperance Hall. The youngsters ate their way through 550 pies, 158 lbs of cake, 4 hams and 30 loaves.

A Rechabite picnic outside the old Institute Pelton Fell. They believed there was an alternative to poor relief and this was self help. The Rechabites were part of the temperance movement and believed drink was one of the causes of poverty. They got their name from the bible – the Rechabites vowed to 'drink no wine all our days, we, our wives, our sons, nor our daughters.'

Diet of the Poor

The inter-war years were a particularly hard time for many in the North East. High unemployment meant families with the wage earner out of work often went hungry. The *New Leader* of 18th January 1929 recalled how an Independent Labour Party reporter found evidence of malnutrition in the Bishop Auckland area: 'Everywhere we saw children – poor pathetic little mites – with legs and arms like matchsticks, thin white faces, and all their natural vitality supped by a constant diet of bread and "marg".'

Suffragettes

In the years leading up to the First World War the Suffragette Movement became increasingly militant in their campaign for votes for women. One of the leading activists in County Durham was Connie Lewcock, née Ellis, from Esh Winning. She came up with a plan to blow up Durham Cathedral. Will Lawther (later to become MP for Barnard Castle) said he could supply the explosives to do the job. At the last minute she decided not to go ahead with the plan because she thought she might blow herself up as well as the Norman cathedral.

Right: A poster showing the ordeal suffragettes on hunger strike in prison had to endure.

Patients being given plenty of fresh air at Holywood Hall Sanatorium at Wolsingham in the 1930s. This was an important part of the recuperation treatment of those suffering from Tuberculosis.

Hungry and Barefoot

GRANGE ROAD, JARROW-ON-TYNE (137)

One of the main streets in Jarrow in the days when some children had to go barefoot.

In her book *The Town That Was Murdered* Ellen Wilkinson MP described the effect unemployment had on families in Jarrow in the 1930s. One large family's staple diet was 'tea, bread, margarine, potatoes, cheap jam, with stew at weekends. The mother is ailing, obviously taking less than her share.' Three of the eight children in the family were certified as being under-nourished and received free meals and milk at the school canteen. Yet this family could consider themselves more fortunate than some in Jarrow at that time. Ellen Wilkinson described how doctor's notes could give mothers an extra two shillings and sixpence a week if the doctor found her or her children suffering from malnutrition.

The end of nineteenth century and the early decades of the twentieth century were hard times for many in County Durham – especially children. In large towns like South Shields and Sunderland various philanthropist groups organised 'boot funds' to buy footwear for children who were going barefoot in the streets. 'Breakfast Funds' were also set up to ensure poor children would have a least one meal a day.

Right: Spring Garden Lane around 1900. Poverty and overcrowding were widespread in this part of Sunderland's East End at this time.

The Days They Gave Away Children

In 1891 the Poor Law Guardians of Lanchester Workhouse received a letter from the Emigration Home for Destitute Little Girls asking them if they would consider sending any of their girls from 9 to 13 years of age to Canada. This was part of a scheme whereby Poor Law Guardians all round the country would pay £8 plus an outfit of clothing for every child that left their Workhouse to be sent overseas.

As well as Workhouse children those from homes run by Dr Barnardo's and church societies also found themselves sent to the places like Australia, New Zealand, South Africa, Rhodesia as well as Canada.

While many children no doubt benefited from a fresh start in a new land others were used as cheap labour or worse.

In their book *Lost Children of the Empire* Philip Bean and Joy Melville revealed how it was

Dr. Barnardo's Homes. Our Young Emigrants.

Barnardo Children at a country School.

A Dr Barnardo card showing how their young emigrants were doing.

the Roman Catholic girls and boys who suffered the most abuse. Girls were hit by nuns for small misdemeanours with leather straps, belts, bamboo canes and in one instance the leg of a wooden chair.

In the years after the war 10,000 children were sent out to Australia – the last in 1967. Many youngsters who had been placed in children's homes after the break-up of their parents' marriage were told that their parents were dead.

If Lanchester Poor Law Guardians had allowed the girls in their care to go to Canada they might have been surprised by their treatment. They could be sent to isolated farms where they would be used as slave labour. Many worked outside from dawn to dusk and in winter had to cope with temperatures as low 40 degrees below zero.

William Booth's vision to establish overseas colonies for the nation's poor and destitute outlined in *In Darkest England & The Way Out* in 1890. 'The Colony Across the Sea' was the place the Salvation Army planned to transport paupers, discharged prisoners and fallen women.

A Way Of Death
by Dorothy A. Rand

From interviews in the Pelton area.

Death was not hidden away in the earlier part of the twentieth century, people died at home, were laid out at home, and in the days between the death and the funeral the corpse and coffin were inspected by visitors. Children were not shielded from this and it would have been impossible anyway.

In the first decade of the century when toddler Violet May Cook died, she was placed, in tribute to her name, in a coffin lined with violet velvet and decorated with May blossom. Her sister remembered seeing this when little more than a toddler herself. Former teacher Elsie Harrison remembers when a frail 12-year-old classmate, Wilhelmina Thirlwell, died in 1926. About a hundred pupils from Roseberry Girls School trooped through the colliery house at Stack Terrace, Newfield, in one door, past the open coffin and out of the other to see Wilhelmina before the funeral. The coffin was carried all the way from Newfield to Pelton Church for a Spiritualist funeral with the schoolgirls and many others following.

Nan Rawling remembers when her friend at Roseberry Girls School was killed in 1933. Nan was playing with Irene Harbottle and her younger sister, when the sister jumped on to a big roller on the pit heap. A lever flew up and killed Irene while her sister was badly injured. The school children brought fruit into school and Nan got the job of taking it to Irene's sister. Nan remembers seeing Irene's corpse with pennies on the eyes and cotton wool in the ears and up the nose.

All of these and other memories were recalled in a matter-of-fact way with no sense of revulsion – the way of death was part of their way of life.

THOMAS HALL,
Cab Proprietor, etc.
MIDDLETON-ONE-ROW,
Nat. Telephone: 21.   **DARLINGTON.**

Cabs and Governess Cars for hire.   Parties catered for.   Funerals furnished.
Mourning Coaches, etc.   All orders receive prompt attention.
Horses taken in at Livery.   Telegrams: "Thomas Hall, Middleton-One-Row."

'Funerals furnished' was one of the services advertised by this Middleton-One-Row cab proprietor in 1913.

Hard Times in Monkwearmouth

by Jessie Robertson

I was born in No 2 Back Stables down beside the Folly End in Monkwearmouth in 1907. I was Josephine Wallace then but I got the name of Jessie and I was one of 22 children my mother had, they did not all grow up, but there was still a lot of us at home. We all lived in two rooms and there were three other families in the building with one toilet in the yard and one tap.

When I went to St Benet's School, one of the sisters there was Sister Mary Clements who was at the school for many years after that. Some of the teachers were Miss Brazil, Miss Barrington and Miss Carty. A lot of my friends in those days had no shoes. I had one set of clothes so my mother would wash them and dry them in the oven for school next day.

My mother had a hard life bringing us all up. She worked at the Ropery in Roker Avenue for terrible long hours for seven shillings (35p) a week. When I look back on it today it was slavery. She would tell me of the girls that had to work in the rubbish pit sorting the bits of sisal from the dust and dirt that was in there. All the girls that did this work are all dead now of bad chests. Some of the girls had to work

St Peter's Church at Monkwearmouth around 1955. The 'Dead House' is to the right of the church. Hall Garth Square stands immediately in front of the church. The Back Stables stood in the foreground right just out of the picture.

A view of Monkwearmouth shore in 1880.

under the machines cleaning the dust and grease under them. They hated the Ropery and one of my mother's friends, Mary Ann Maguire, had her arm pulled off while my mother was there.

At the end of her working day she would go to the wash house at the bottom of Church Street and take people's clothes there and poss them for three pence just to feed.

One memory was of my mother going down to the big houses on Roker front to see if there was any food to be thrown out and she would collect it and bring it home for us.

She would send me down to Lumsdon's butchers or Alf Harrison's to get a bag of bones to make soup for a few days.

When we were girls I would shovel the miners' ton of coal into the coal house through the hatch from the street where it was tipped. In return for this work I was given a couple of pails of coal to help keep the fire on. I remember pushing a pram full of tarry blocks for the fire from Roker Avenue down to Hardwick Street when they tarred the street.

I knew where every pawnshop in Monkwearmouth was in those days. I think I was in them all. Gowdy had a few, the one in Gladstone Street had cubicles where you could do your pawning in private. One of my uncles used to pawn his new cap every week for two bob (10p) and get it out again for the weekend. My brother was a coppersmith and would make rings from a penny for the women who had pawned their wedding rings. He must have made hundreds. Its surprising how many women wore copper rings made from a penny that no one knew about.

When I was young we would go and watch them bringing the bodies from the river, put them on a barrow and wheel them to the Dead House. It was where the vicar's house for St Peter's is now.

They talk about the good old days, there was no good times in Monkwearmouth then, but it seems no one wants to know about that, the good days are now.

A DAY TO REMEMBER

A Special St Patrick's Day
by Ann Nora Robinson (née Henderson)

Every year there was a St Patrick's dance held in the Rink dance hall in Sunderland. It was a very popular venue and the tickets were like gold. As the 1940s were a time when the country was at war everyone looked forward to a good night out. As I had attended St Patrick's School and I was a parishioner of St Patrick's Roman Catholic Church, acquiring tickets was no problem. So, if any of my friends wanted tickets all they needed to do was to ask me.

One evening one of my friends asked if he could possibly have two tickets for the dance. This was unusual for Albert as he normally only bought one ticket as we all just met inside the dance hall. He explained that the ticket was for his friend who had never been to the St Patrick's dance and as Albert had always told him what a great night it was he would like to come. I gave him the two tickets next time I saw him and he told me that his friend did appreciate the fact that I had obtained a ticket for him.

On the night of the dance I was with my friends when Albert walked in with his friend. They both came over and I was introduced to his friend, George Robinson. George then asked me how much he owed me for the ticket. I told him the price of the ticket was one dance during the evening.

When George did ask me to dance we realised that we only lived streets away from each other but our paths had never crossed. At the time he lived in Moor Street and I lived in Woodbine Street. We started going out from that moment and as many other couples did when they realised that their courting was 'serious' I took George home to meet my mother, as my father had died when I was only eleven years old.

Myself – This photograph was taken in Jeromes in High Street.

George – The photograph he sent me as a keepsake.

My four-year-old niece, Theresa, also lived with my mother and I in Woodbine Street, so on Sunday afternoon George was invited for the traditional 'Sunday Tea'. As it was a special occasion there was shop-bought cream cakes. This was certainly a treat as rationing made such things quite a luxury. Everything was going well, the conversation over the tea table was light-hearted and everyone seemed to be enjoying themselves that was until George picked up a second cream cake from the plate on the table. 'He is eating all the bestest cakes!' screamed my niece, George promptly dropped the cake back on the plate. No one could speak for a moment or two. My mother

Our family – Jimmy, Ann and Margaret on our way home from Mowbray Park in 1956.

was quite annoyed at my niece as children at that time were to be seen and not heard! But George did see the funny side but vowed never to choose a cream cake before Theresa had picked the 'bestest' one, and he never allowed Theresa to forget her outburst!

George was a corporal in the Royal Signals and when he went back to the Army we carried on our courtship throughout the rest of the war and beyond. We sent photographs to each other along with our letters. We were married in March 1951 at St Patrick's Church while George was still in the Army. He was serving in Egypt at the time and had just been promoted to sergeant. When he next came home on leave he asked me if I would go back with him to Egypt and live in married quarters, but I wanted to stay at home as I could not bear to be so far away from my mother. George understood and when it came to the end of his leave he decided not to re-enlist when the time came.

The clearance of the old East End continued over a number of years. This is Hartley Street meeting its end in the 1960s.

Over the years we had a family of one boy and three girls, we did not move away from Woodbine Street or my mother. We were re-housed when the council began demolishing the old houses in Hendon and the East End in 1958.

We both attended the last mass celebrated in St Patrick's Roman Catholic Church on 4th December 1984 and said our last goodbyes to the church where our married life began all those years ago.

The Lady Who Gave Up Her Seat
(For Her Husband)
by Lily Brett

The 8th February 1929 was certainly a red letter day in the life of Ruth Dalton for on that day she was declared Member of Parliament for Bishop Auckland, having doubled Labour's majority from the previous General Election. However, this was not first step on a glittering political career but a remarkable effort to enable her husband to take her place a few months later.

Hugh Dalton was MP for Peckham when the sitting MP for Bishop Auckland, Ben Spoor, announced he would not be seeking re-election. Dalton decided to try to become the candidate for this safe Labour seat (he had lost four elections before winning Peckham). He was interviewed and chosen in October 1928 to fight the General Election sometime in the following year.

Only a couple of months later the sudden death of Spoor threw the plan into turmoil. For Dalton to fight a by-election at Bishop Auckland would not only mean another by-election at Peckham but as the new

Ruth Dalton using an oxy-acetylene torch on railings in London in 1941. She was helping the campaign to collect scrap for the war effort.

candidate chosen to fight Peckham was also a sitting MP a total of three would have to be held. This tricky problem was solved by Ruth Dalton contesting the seat and, if elected, would then give up the seat when the next General Election was held only months later.

During her campaigning in the constituency Ruth was shocked by what she found. She recalled: 'Everywhere we noticed women who looked haggard and ill, who were obviously facing semi-starvation themselves in order that their families might have, not enough (for no one has enough in the coalfields these days) but as much as possible, to eat.'

On Election Day the voters gave her a ringing endorsement – her 14,797 votes was over 7,000 more than the Liberal candidate received.

Her parliamentary career was to last only three months. When the General Election was announced for May 1929 she duly stepped aside so her husband could contest the seat.

While Hugh Dalton went on to rise through the Government ranks, becoming Chancellor of the Exchequer in 1945, Ruth combined helping her husband in his Bishop Auckland constituency with a career in local politics in London.

During the 1950 General Election Ruth was still helping her husband's campaign by sending out a message to women in the constituency.

A Message to the Women Electors of the Bishop Auckland Division.

I appeal to you all to support my husband for two reasons.

First – Because, thanks to his personal initiative and continuous effort this Division has been transformed from a Distressed Area full of under-nourished and ill-clad men, women and children into a prosperous Development Area, giving regular employment in its new factories to thousands of adults and juveniles.

Second – Because, *thanks to the Labour Government*, mothers receive more help than ever before for themselves and their families, through maternity benefits, more generous maternity and child welfare services, free milk for all schoolchildren, more equal educational opportunities, family allowances and last but not least, the great National Health Service.

Vote Labour, so that all this grand work may go on.

Ruth Dalton

This plea to women voters might have gone some way to help the return of Hugh Dalton as Bishop Auckland MP. He received 25,039 votes – 11,370 more than the Conservative candidate who finished second.

Coronation Day

The Coronation in 1953 led to a huge increase in television sales. Families and friends huddled around their tiny black and white sets on the big day.

An advertisement for a Coronation Carnival Ball to be held at the Seaburn Hall and the interior of the dance hall (*below*).

The inclement weather on Coronation Day forced street parties indoors. Church halls, community centres and school halls were all pressed into service. People in Sunderland found some unconventional ways to beat the downpour. The children from one street party decamped

to a wholesale fruiterer's warehouse in Back Carley Road. The children had their tea and games amongst the sacks of apples and oranges. Perhaps the strangest event was held in a removal van. To escape the rain, tables were set up in the van and the party was held undercover. Luckily the driver lived in the street where the party was supposed to be held.

Residents lighting candles at Burleigh Garth in Sunderland's East End for the Coronation in 1953. The plan was for all the tenants in the blocks of flats to put candles on their balconies so they could be seen miles out to sea. However, on Coronation Day rain washed-out many of the entertainments.

The *Sunderland Echo* reported:

NO CANDLES

'In the heart of the near-silent East End there might have been candles – thousands of them – twinkling from the balconies. There might have been singing and dancing in the squares below.

Instead a few fairy lights glowed from rain-spattered windows, a handful of children – "Spanish Ladies" they called themselves – bravely sang a snatch of song, then disappeared into the darkness, surrendering to the elements.'

Two of Sunderland's East End Garths where residents tried to hold their own special celebration for the Coronation.

Special Days in Church
by Esther Meechin

I used to attend All Saints Parish Church at Wheatley Hill twice on a Sunday. There was the morning service with the grown-ups and the afternoon service for us children. The grown-ups had another service in the evenings but I was only allowed to go to that one after I was confirmed. Ma encouraged us to go to church but she never forced us to go. I liked going to church and it was always full. We had to get there early to get a seat and they

A scene in the back yard of 15 Pyman Street, Wheatley Hill, in 1935. The occasion was the Confirmation Day of Esther Meechin (left) who is wearing her Confirmation dress. Next to Esther are her sisters Jean and Margaret (right). The lads at the back are from the left, John Watson, Tom Meechin and Alf Watson.

The Wedding Day of Esther Meechin and Jimmy Gibson on 29th July 1950. The couple were married in the Church of the English Martyrs at Thornley. There wasn't a Catholic Church at the bride's village of Wheatley Hill.

would put extra chairs down the side aisles. Mr Casey, the vicar, was well liked and he was an interesting speaker – everybody said so. We were given a book and each time we attended the morning service we were given a stamp with a religious scene on it to stick into the book. At the afternoon service a star was stamped into the same book. Every year we had a party and the child with the most stamps and stars and cleanest book was awarded the Vicar's Prize which was a good story book. Our Tom was a regular winner of the Vicar's Prize.

The Day War Broke Out & Victory Day
by Mary Robinson

My early childhood in the 1930s, although lean years, were happy times. By the time the year 1939 came around we had already experienced years of rumour of war and then it became a reality. I first learnt war had broken out when I saw placards and newspapers giving out details. People talking, neighbours telling each other the latest bulletins but not understanding the seriousness of it all. Yet life carried on. Adults from our area were employed on munitions, some moving away, others joining the services and even at my young age, I could sense the change around me. The black-outs, ARP (Air Raid Precaution) Wardens taking over our schools to learn how to deal with First Aid etc. We children were moved into accommodation of private homes to help out with our normal lessons. Air Raids became more frequent and bombing heavier from 1940 onwards. We were sometimes stuck in a brick air raid shelter for the best part of the night. In our street the shelter was built at the side way of our home. Many families evacuated their children to safe areas. Many stayed at home. We young got used to shortages of almost everything. Ration books for clothing, food, sweets and fruits, yet our parents did without to supply we young with small treats of toffee apples, cakes, cinder toffee etc. Our games were played around our streets. A special delight was a Sunday School trip to some out-lying place with a few prizes to be won and a bag of cakes and orangeade. We arrived home early evening tired out after all that lovely fresh air with plenty to talk about to take our minds off the bombing raids.

My teenage years were spent through those six years of war and as children we saw devastation of homes and death. The radio and local picture halls were main stay pastimes that kept our spirits up and it seemed to we young the war was never ending. Yet in one sense our country was fortunate when we learned of how other countries had suffered.

I'll never forget the voice of Prime Minister Churchill speaking to the British nation on Victory Day. It made me feel so proud, and now at the age of sweet 17 I joined the crowds in the streets and danced with them. It was a time never to forget.

Mary Robinson at the end of the war in Roker Park.

Memories of Christmas at Burnopfield
by Dorothy A. Rand

The earliest preparations in our house were making the Christmas puddings and cake. The puddings were made to a wartime recipe which resulted in a lighter, less rich pudding. Mam liked this so much she used this recipe for another forty years! It included breadcrumbs made by baking slices of bread in the oven and then crushing them with a rolling pin. Another ingredient was grated carrot. The smell of the cake baking in the oven was wonderful. I loved to watch Mam decorating the cake, she made marzipan from ground almonds and egg yolks. Any trimmings left over became my property. I used dates and walnuts to make sweets. I was also allowed to decorate biscuits with leftover white icing, using the icing tube to pipe 'stars'.

The anticipation was very exciting. Before Christmas Day itself we had our school party. We had to take sixpence, plus a cup, plate and spoon. Mam was always terrified I wouldn't get my own things back. She stuck cloth elastoplast strips on my cup and plate with my name on in Biro (Biros were new then). She wrapped coloured wool around my spoon handle so that it could be identified. I took these to school in a brown paper bag. The teas were set out with identical items on each plate. Party activities were dances and games such as *The Grand Old Duke of York*, *In And Out The Dusty Bluebells*, *The Farmer Wants A Wife* and *Musical Chairs*.

A family tradition was to keep the Christmas cake until cutting it at midnight on New Year's Eve. The Christmas cake is on the table and Ena Noble can be seen pouring ginger wine watched by daughter Dorothy.

The school party ended with the distribution of cards from the post box in the hall. One poor boy in my class, rather backward, did not receive a single card. One of the teachers took pity on him and went to the staff room to get a card from all of the staff to him. I vaguely remember that when paper was so short some

Dorothy Rand in the spectacular winter of 1947. Not only is she holding a Christmas present but she is also wearing some as well.

people re-used Christmas cards by using bleach on the original writing.

It was easy for me to be excited about Christmas but it meant extra work for my mother. Christmas preparations did not start so early then, presents were bought locally or made at home. One year – 1949 or 1950 – my mother sent for a Samuel Drivers catalogue and ordered several items, including a bottle of Egg Flip. I don't to this day know what is in Egg Flip. My parents were Sons of Temperance and strict teetotallers. Our cat took one whiff of it, I can still see her, in front of the coal scuttle, lapping Egg Flip from her saucer.

We didn't put our decorations up until maybe the day before Christmas Eve. Dad particularly loved the decorations and all the festivity of Christmas, possibly because he'd been born on Christmas Eve in 1905. Grandma said he'd spoilt her Christmas dinner that year! He liked as much as possible draped around the living room, there were no Christmas lights for us, they came soon after 1950.

My grandparents' Christmas decorations, mostly bought in the 1890s, were sent for me. They were, and still are in a wooden box from a shop, used to deliver blacking from the manufacturer. The main decorations are a large bronze-coloured heavy glass bauble and a bright pink swan decorated with a blue-robed Santa. There were many others plus lovely red and green chenille wall drapes trimmed with silver bells.

Before Christmas Day all tradesmen who called at the house had to be caught and given their 'Christmas box' about two shillings at this time. The same people were also invited in for cake and wine on their first visit after New Year.

The food on Christmas Day was entirely different to the rest of the year. Chicken was then a luxury to be had once a year, for Christmas. Mam worried about chickens. The giblets were immediately discarded then she washed the carcass thoroughly inside and out, pulling out any loose bits from the cavity. She did not stuff the chicken, but cooked the stuffing separately. She made it from chopped boiled onions, white breadcrumbs and sage crumbled from a bunch of dried sage bought at the Co-op greengrocers. I looked forward in due course, to being given the wishbone.

With the chicken and stuffing we had potatoes, sprouts and turnip, followed by Christmas pudding and white sauce. After all of this we didn't want much tea. We had the blackberry tart, the Christmas cake was not to be cut into until New Year. We were, like the chicken, well roasted at Christmas, in the small room the table was very near the oven, and dad had kept very large pieces of coal to one side for Christmas.

I was never disappointed with my presents, I always had the main present of my choice and many others besides. My parents were not well off but they took a great deal of time and trouble over my presents. I realised that I had much more than them, the highlight of my dad's childhood Christmas had been a cheap tin toy, soon broken and my mam's was a bar of chocolate and a sugar mouse. My presents were kept in a large wicker laundry basket, behind the rarely-used front door and brought out to display to visitors whom I'd try to inveigle into playing some of the games with me – maybe Snap or Happy Families, Snakes and Ladders, Ludo or Dominoes. There was no TV then to distract, the focus was on people.

Christmas Day always had a lovely warm feeling, a physical and mental warmth pervaded the day. Mam, like many housewives, said she liked Boxing Day better, it was a relief to get Christmas safely over, have a long lie and a leftover dinner.

Then it was on to less hectic preparations for New Year – New Year's Day meant pork for dinner. Before midnight mats were shaken, the ashes taken out, and then it was time to go to the back door to listen to the bells of Byermoor Catholic Church ring in the New Year. Cousin Stan, being dark-haired, was first foot, bearing a piece of coal for good luck. Then there was ginger wine and Christmas cake and it was time for bed. They started the year secure in the knowledge that all bills, even very small ones had been paid. They wanted to start the New Year on the basis of not owing any money (except their mortgage).

Everything was done according to tradition, without deviation. My toys were dispersed from the laundry basket and dad, who loved the decorations, was sad to see them come down on Twelfth Night to be packed away in their large wicker hamper.

POST SCRIPT I still have that wicker hamper with its blacking box of Victorian Christmas decorations, and the mistletoe hoops. One day, when my granddaughter is old enough, I will tell her about the first owners of these things and maybe we will make paper chains and a mistletoe together. I will show her my doll's house, cot and pram and other simple, home-made toys and tell her their story, not forgetting the reason for the giving of gifts, the story of the first Christmas.

Christmas being celebrated at Ryhope General Hospital.

Ferryhill Village Women's Institute pantomime held in the Masonic Hall, Ferryhill in 1972. Some of the youngsters who took part include: Marie McDonald, Stephanie Varty and the Marshall sisters.

Christmas decorations adorn Pease's Mill in Darlington just after the Second World War.

A nativity scene performed by Broom Infants, Ferryhill, 1976. Amongst those taking part are: Kelly Porter, Wendy Cook, Alexandra Knaggs, Catherine Lowey, Catherine Pym, Jane Stayman and Elaine Gibson.

No matter how poor families were, parents made great efforts to make Christmas special for their children. Even if they could not afford big presents they would try their best even if this just meant a stocking full of nuts, fruit and small toys.

Some mothers would join Christmas clubs in toy shops or department stores like Woolworth's. They would go in every week to pay a shilling or so then take their children to the shop just before Christmas to choose their presents.

Right: Annuals were a popular Christmas gift. As well as *School Friend* other favourites included *Diana*, *Bunty*, *Judy* and *The Broons*.

Acknowledgements

The authors would like to thank all of those kind enough to share their memories and photographs with the rest of us:

Joyce Allan, Lily Brett, Nellie Burrell, Joyce Carlson née Wilkinson, Lena Cooper, Phil Curtis, Mrs E. Davies, Bessie Dewey née Failes, Ethel Dickinson, Anne Dixon, Lilian Dixon, Margaret Foulk, Jack Hedley, Margaret Ann Henderson née Mallon, Brian Holden, Tom Hutchinson, Dorothy Jameson née Pearson, Anthea Lang, Jack Laydon, Olive Linge, Chris Lloyd, Esther Meechin, Matty Morrison, George Nairn, Pat O'Brien, Jim & Joan Pace, Miss Parkin, Doris Predki née McLean, Ken Price, Dorothy A. Rand, Jessie Robertson, Ann Nora Robinson née Henderson, Mary Robinson, Martin Routledge, Ashley Sutherland, Alan Tedder, Murdina Tedder née Butler, Avis Tucker, Ann Tyrens, William Tyrens, Anne Varty, Ruth Vickery, Jim Wetherill, Michael White, Peter White, Katherine Williamson, Trevor Williamson and Jane Wooton.

Special thanks to:

Coats Crafts UK for permission to use the picture of Patons and Baldwins.

Darlington Library for photographs and information.

Gateshead Library for permission to use photographs and information from the Tom Marshall Collection.

The Northern Echo for permission to use photographs and information for the article 'Aycliffe Angels'.

Sunderland Echo for information and photographs.

Mr J. Templeton for permission to use the picture of 'Carlisle Market Place' from his Collection.

'The Three Rs' by Miss Parkin first appeared in *But The World Goes On The Same* in 1979.

'The Summer of 1940' by Jane Wooton is an abridged version of an article that first appeared in the August 1979 edition of *Southwick St Hilda's Parish Magazine*.

'Memories of Christmas at Burnopfield' by Dorothy A. Rand is an abridged version of an article that first appeared in *People & Places of Old County Durham* Winter 2000.

'A Way of Death' by Dorothy A. Rand first appeared in *People & Places of Old County Durham* Autumn 2000.

Bibliography

Frank Atkinson *Life and Traditions in Northumberland & Durham* J.M. Dent 1977

Philip Bean and Joy Melville *Lost Children Of The Empire*, Hyman 1989

R. Bell *Twenty-Five Years of the North Eastern Railway* 1898-1922 Railway Gazette 1951

William Booth *In Darkest England & The Way Out* 1890

John Brewster *History of Stockton upon Tees* 1829

Hugh Dalton *High Tide And After – Memoirs 1945-1960* Frederick Muller 1962

Lilian Dixon *Lanchester in Times Past* Countryside Publications 1987

Lilian Dixon *More About Lanchester* l. Dixon 1989

William Fordyce *Histories and Antiquities of the County Palatine of Durham* Fullerton 1857

George S. Hearse *The Tramways of Jarrow And South Shields* 1971

Norman McCord *North East England – The Region's Development 1760-1960* Batsford Academic 1979

Norman McCord and Richard Thompson *The Northern Counties from AD 1000* Longman 1998

John Lee *Weardale Memories and Traditions*

F.W.D. Manders *A History of Gateshead* Gateshead Corporation 1973

Christopher Martin *English Life in the First World War* Wayland 1974

R. Martin *Historical Notes of West Hartlepool and its Founder* Robert Martin 1924

Arthur Marwick *Women At War* Croom Helm 1977

Matty Morrison *Sunderland Tramways to Busways* Black Cat Publications 2001

John Ryan *History of Shotley Spa* Vint & Carr 1841

S.A. Staddon *The Tramways of Sunderland* The Advertiser Press 1964

John Sykes *Local Records or Historical Register of Remarkable Events* 1866

Ellen Wilkinson *The Town That Was Murdered* Victor Gollancz 1939

Birth Counts – Statistics of Pregnancy and Childbirth The Stationery Office *2000*

Annfield Plain Co-operative Industrial Society Jubilee Souvenir 1870-1920

But The World Goes On The Same Strong Words 1979

Trade Directories	Journals & Magazines	Newspapers
Bennett's,	People & Places of Old County Durham	Daily Express
Kelly's,	Punch	Northern Echo
Slater's	Radio Times	Seaham Observer
Ward's	Southwick St Hilda's Parish Magazine	Seaham Weekly News
	Town Guides	Sunderland Echo

Ladies enjoying a cuppa in a front garden of a house in Southwick.

The People's History

To receive a catalogue of our latest titles send a large SAE to:

The People's History
Suite 1
Byron House
Seaham Grange Business Park
Seaham
County Durham
SR7 0PY

www.thepeopleshistory.co.uk